Ready or Not

Here I Come!

Robert L. Bradley

Robert L. Bradley
Rev 22:20

1663 Liberty Drive, Suite 200
Bloomington, Indiana 47403
(800) 839-8640
www.AuthorHouse.com

© 2005 Robert L. Bradley. All Rights Reserved.

No part of this book may be reproduced, stored in a retrieval system, or transmitted by any means without the written permission of the author.

First published by AuthorHouse 11/29/05

ISBN: 1-4208-8742-4 (sc)

Library of Congress Control Number: 2005908547

Printed in the United States of America
Bloomington, Indiana

This book is printed on acid-free paper.

Acknowledgements

I want to thank the following people for their encouragement and help to make this book possible:

- Joan K. Bradley, my dear daughter-in-law, wife of our son Bruce, who has spent many hours of her busy time editing my book and whose professional expertise gave me a more comprehensive perspective of the material in my book.

- Sharon B. Miller, who urged me to write long before I made the attempt, and who, along with Mary L. DeMott, gave suggestions and ideas that were very helpful in setting up the book.

- And I never could have completed the task without the encouragement and support of my dear, loving wife, Virginia, who carried out the daily correspondence needed, offered helpful suggestions, and critiqued my book page by page, and is still my best friend.

- And to all those who will read this book and be challenged enough to change in order to be ready for Christ's return.

- And lastly, to my Lord and Savior, who birthed this book in my heart.

Bible Translations Used:

Unless indicated all scriptures were taken from the:

- NKJV New King James Version
    Copyright 1996
    Broadman & Holman Publishers

All other versions are indicated when used in the text:

- NIV New International Version
    Copyright 1996
    Broadman & Holman Publishers

- KJV King James Version
    Copyright 1964
    B.B. Kirkbride Bible Company., Inc.

- Msg The Message//Remix
    Copyright 2003
    Eugene Peterson

Table of Contents

Acknowledgements	v
Bible Translations Used:	vii
Introduction	xi
01–Derailed	1
02–Fading Affection	13
03–Caught in the Current	25
04–Facing Our Fall	37
05–Slipping To Substitutes	47
06–Wake-Up Call	57
07–Judgment Begins At Home!	65
08–Shaken Loose!	75
09–Blessed Affliction	87
10–Are You Ready?	97
Resources Used	105

Introduction

God has a plan and purpose for everything He does here on earth. **"The Lord Almighty has sworn, 'Surely as I have planned, so it will be, and as I have purposed, so it will stand.'"** Isaiah 14:24 (NIV). For you and me to be a part of that great plan is the greatest honor bestowed upon mortal humans.

God opened to me His plan and purpose for my life in 1953 when He called me to preach the gospel. During a normal Sunday evening church service in the Assembly of God Church in Boyne City, Michigan, Pastor Bill Severance had just finished preaching and people were assembled around the altar for a time of prayer. As I knelt at the altar, I was doing some deep soul searching and reflective praying when, suddenly, the power of God hit me and I was prostrated on my face seemingly nailed to the floor. I lay there, conscious of what was going on around me yet unable to move a muscle. I remember thinking, "I can't even lift my fingers because I am so totally overpowered by God." I was so completely absorbed by God I had no concept of time. Then it happened! God spoke to my heart. It was neither an audible voice nor a booming thunder from heaven but an inner revelation that swept over my whole being enlightening me to the fact that God had called me to preach His word. After that very intimate experience with God, it seemed that His power catapulted me to my feet. I began to run around the church exclaiming, "God has called me to preach, God has called me to preach!" This was so far from my character that I knew that it was of God. Yes, I was called to preach the gospel, but down deep in the portals of my understanding there was a further unfolding of God's call to me. **The specific mission was to prepare God's people for His coming.**

At that time, I didn't know the full implications of God's call but it has stuck with me for more than 50 years. I often have doubted my salvation more than I have doubted the particulars of God's call on my life. God knew that I was the type of person who would give up easily if I wasn't sure of what I was supposed to do. He made sure that I knew His purpose for me beyond any shadow of any doubt. Today, this call and purpose are as real to me as they were the day they were given.

Preparing God's people for His coming is a demanding task and one I would never want to tackle without the calling and enabling of the Lord. It's the message that the Prophets were entrusted with – they often were stoned or killed for bringing it to the people!

As the years have passed, I have felt an acceleration of the urgency of this calling. I know that Jesus is coming soon! Although the vast majority of Christians believe this, few are doing anything about it. No doubt you are among those who would agree that Jesus is coming soon. Has it changed your lifestyle? Has it challenged you to pray more? Are you witnessing more than you ever have? Are you ready to welcome the coming of the Lord today? Are there things you would want to change before you had to face God? It is time we began to live like we really believed that the Lord's coming is imminent.

I remember as a child when we played 'hide and seek' that one of us would have to cover our eyes while the rest hid. The one who had their eyes covered would keep calling out, "Are you ready, are you ready?" If there was no response he or she would finally announce, "Ready or not, here I come."

Picture with me, if you can, God standing, perhaps at the Tree of Life, with His head bent and His eyes covered and counting down through the years…"2000, 2001, 2002, 2003, 2004, 200?," then lifting His head and calling out, "Ready or Not, Here I come!"

It's time to get ready because He has said, "I'm on my way! I'll be there soon!" Can you say with John, *"Yes! Come, Master Jesus?"* Revelation 22:20 (Msg)

God's message to us is, **"Ready or not, here I come."**

DERAILED
Chapter 1

*"Husbands, love your wives, even as Christ also
loved the church, and gave himself for it;
That he might sanctify and cleanse it with the
washing of water by the word,
That he might present it to himself a glorious church,
not having spot, or wrinkle, or any such thing but
that it should be holy and without blemish."*
EPHESIANS 5:25-27 (KJV)

On January 28, 1986, only a little over a minute after lift-off, the space shuttle, "Challenger," exploded before the eyes of millions of spectators, leaving seven families mourning the loss of a loved one. The entire nation stood in shock over this horrifying incident. The cause for this multi-million dollar calamity was found to be an inexpensive O-ring. The shuttle was composed of more than one million working parts that were responsible to get the shuttle lifted off as scheduled. But, when one small part failed to do its task, the entire mission was compromised and destroyed.

Many people within the Church, feel that their function is trivial and inconsequential. They fail to recognize that every member of the church is indispensable, and without them, our mission to reach the world with the gospel, will be limited.

The Church of Jesus Christ is a glorious wonder, instituted and implemented by the Holy Spirit to become the Bride of Christ.

We can understand this being expressed in the enduring hymn of Ralph E. Hudson, "A Glorious Church." It has been a source of blessing and inspiration to me for many years. Notice the challenging words in this hymn:

"Do you hear them coming brother, thronging up the steeps of light?
Clad in glorious shining garments, blood-
washed garments pure and white?
Do you hear the stirring anthems filling all the earth and sky,
'Tis a grand victorious army, lift its banner up on high!
Never fear the clouds of sorrow, never fear the storms of sin;
We shall triumph on the morrow, even now our joys begin.
Wave the banners, shout His praises, for our victory is nigh!
We shall join our conquering Savior, we shall reign with Him on high!
'Tis a glorious Church without spot or wrinkle,
washed in the blood of the lamb;
'Tis a glorious Church without spot or wrinkle,
washed in the blood of the Lamb."(6)

I am thrilled to know that I am a part of that "Glorious Church" of Jesus Christ and able to participate with Him in His work on earth today.

When I refer to the "Church," I am speaking of those who claim to be Christians and representatives of Christ. And, particularly I am speaking about the church in America today.

The record of the birth of the church in the book of Acts gives us a blow by blow account of how it began, grew, and developed. Just think… it was a pioneer church that had 3,000 converts at the very first service they held. (Acts 2:41) From there we read how the Lord added to the church daily. (Acts 2:47) By the time we come to Acts 4:4, we find the number had grown to 5,000 men. (Wow! What a men's fellowship group!) There certainly was unity in that church because people sold what they possessed and gave to those who had a need. (Acts 4:34) It seemed that nothing would be able to stop this "Glorious Church."

Whether those early Christians knew it or not, they were in a battle against the powers of Satan. They were attacked on every front and experienced casualties along the way. Persecution was common and some church leaders were thrown into prison. The persecution caused the saints to cloister in already evangelized cities rather than scattering to spread the gospel.

There were also battles within the ranks of these early Christians as some of them yielded to greed and withheld of their contributions to God.

Others favored supporting only widows of their own nationality. So we see; the problems became even more complex.

During the Civil War, a Union soldier from Ohio was shot in the arm. His captain saw he was wounded and barked out an order.

"Gimme your gun, Private, and get to the rear."

The private handed over his rifle and ran toward the north, seeking safety. But, after going about 200 to 300 yards, he came upon another skirmish. So, he ran to the east and found himself in yet another part of the battle. Then he ran west, but encountered more fighting. Finally, he ran back to the front lines shouting,

*"Gimme back my rifle, Cap'n. There ain't no
rear to this battle nowhere!" (1)*

It seems that there "ain't no rear to this battle" against evil either. The years have come and gone and the battle rages on. The "Glorious Church" has been criticized, plagiarized, traumatized, scandalized, customized, modernized, and compromised. Along the way, the old "Gospel Ship" has taken some direct hits and has begun to leak here and there.

It is not the external opposition that is hurting the Church; in fact, it would seem where the external opposition is the most strenuous, the Church is the strongest. In countries where there is the most severe persecution, you will find the purest and strongest of Christians found anywhere. It is the contamination within the Church that steadily drags us to a lower spiritual level. If the Church is to become the evangelizing force that God intended, it will have to cleanse itself from within. Although there are problems in the Church today, we have the ability to make choices to resolve them and to move in the direction of revival.

James gave us good instruction. (James 4:1-2) He talks about fights and quarrels and that they come about because people want their own way. He talks about wrong motives in prayer, because people are like spoiled children wanting what they want. He tells them that they are cheating on God and flirting with the world.

James was addressing Christians, not sinners. Then James goes on to say:

"So let God work His will in you. Yell a loud "no" to the Devil and watch him scamper. Say a quiet "yes" to God and He'll be there in no time. Quit dabbling in sin. Purify your inner life. Quit playing the field. Hit bottom and cry you eyes out. The fun and games are over. Get serious, really serious. Get down on your knees before the Master; it's the only way you'll get on your feet."
James 4:7-10 (Msg)

One has to admit that James gives some very practical teaching on what is needed in the Church if it is to become the "Glorious Church" once again. He had to expose backslidden and derailed Christians who were far from being what God intended His "Glorious Church" to be.

Paul warned Timothy that we would face increasingly difficult and troublesome times:

"The Spirit clearly says that in the later times some will abandon the faith and follow deceiving spirits and things taught by demons."
I Timothy 4:1-3 (NIV)

Obviously Paul has in mind here, people who were believers at one time in their lives. You can't abandon something you have never embraced. These are the conditions that will exist in the later times, or in the last days involving God's people, and we can see it happening today.

"Don't be naïve. There are difficult times ahead. As the end approaches, people are going to be self-absorbed, money-hungry, self-promoting, stuck-up, profane, contemptuous of parents, crude, coarse, dog-eat-dog, unbending, slanderers, impulsively wild, savage, cynical, treacherous, ruthless, bloated windbags, addicted to lust, and allergic to God. They'll make a show of religion, but behind the scenes they're animals. Stay clear of these people."
II Timothy 3:1-5 (Msg)

One only has to look around him and see that these conditions are in full bloom today. The truth that stands out to me is the fact that they will, "Make a show of religion." The King James Version says, "Having a form of godliness." I don't think I would call these people Christians, but they call themselves Christians.

I am appalled at what passes as "Christian" today. Ask the average American person if he is a Christian, and you will get a "yes" from a majority. Ask that person what makes them a Christian, and they will, in the majority of cases, give you some form of an answer that describes them as having more good in them than bad. Follow that person through a week of their lives, and you will find much of what Paul portrays for us in II Timothy 3:1-5 is practiced in their lives.

All of this is affecting the Church of Jesus Christ. Standards for the Church have been reduced to an all-time low, accommodating the trends of the world. The divorce rate in the church is as high as in our present society. People are losing confidence in the integrity of the Church in light of the many scandals surfacing today. Acts of self sacrifice are growing scarcer. It is more common to hear of jealousy, pride, gossip, and injustice than to hear of unselfish deeds being done by Christians. What were once the standards of the world have become the standards of the Church. I shudder to think what will happen if the Church continues in these trends and does not wake up and get back on track with God.

Paul expounds on this problem in Romans.

> *"And be not conformed to this world, but be transformed by the renewing of your mind..."*
>
> Romans 12:2a (KJV)

The Greek word here for "conformed" means to "fashion alike, to conform to a pattern." This tells us that the world is trying to squeeze Christians into the same pattern as they, the world, are molded. Sadly, one has to admit that the Church is becoming more and more like the world. **The Church no longer sets the standards for the world.** The world sets the standards for the Church. Instead of the world becoming more like the church, the Church is becoming more like the world. Righteousness is not spreading into the world from the Church, but sin is spreading into the Church from the world.

To counter this pressure to conform to the world, Paul instructs us to rather be transformed by the renewing of our minds. The Greek word for transformed is "metamorphoo" from which we get our word "metamorphosis" which is the process that makes a tadpole into a frog. It is not an external change that affects the internal, but an internal change that affects the external.

Once we have had this spiritual metamorphosis and have been changed from the inside out, we have to maintain this experience, or we are in danger of losing it.

There are two ways to keep a diesel truck running. The first is called "troubleshooting and repair" and involves waiting for a breakdown and then trying to fix the problem. This involves so much downtime however, that most truckers now use the "preventive maintenance" approach, in which problems are anticipated and thus solved before they occur. (3)

Most of us are aware of the provision made for the Christians who have a spiritual breakdown; that if we confess our sins God will forgive us and cleanse us. (I John 1:9) How much better it would be if we would learn to use the 'preventive maintenance' approach and retain a close walk with God every day.

It's so easy to get caught in the current of plummeting trends and be carried further and further from God and the standards He has prescribed for us in His Word. When we have drifted far enough to be startled at our own condition, then we quickly resort to I John 1:9 and ask God to fix our breakdown.

We are, however, instructed in I John:

"But if we walk in the light, as He is in the light, we have fellowship one with another, and the blood of Jesus Christ His Son, cleanseth us from all sin."
I John 1:7 (KJV)

Walking in the light means that we obey the truth of His Word and maintain a consistent relationship with Him. When we do this, we will avoid a breakdown and elude the need to repent and be fixed.

There are not enough Christians who are maintaining a consistent relationship with God in these last days. This is fulfillment of prophesy:

"..for that day shall not come, except there come a falling away..."
II Thessalonians 2:3 (KJV)

Strong's Concordance defines the "falling away" as a defection from truth. Wycliffe's Bible Commentary defines it as a rebellion. This commentary goes on to say, **"The reference here is probably to the marshalling of the powers of evil against the people and purposes of God."** It is not difficult to see from this that there is a battle going on to draw God's people away from Him and defile them in the things of sinful flesh. Satan is behind this, and since He cannot effectively do battle against God, he turns to the Children of God and seeks to do injury to God by inflicting casualties among God's people.

In the midst of the end-times signs that Jesus foretells will take place, He says:

*"And because iniquity [sin] shall abound,
the love of many shall wax cold."*

Matthew 24:12 (KJV)

The best way that Satan has to lure God's people away from God is to cause sin to abound in such a manner that Christians will feel ill at ease in a permissive environment. They then begin to conform to the pattern of the world around them in order to fit in.

According to a radio report, a middle school in Oregon faced a unique problem in that a number of girls began to use lipstick, applying it in the bathroom. After they put on their lipstick, they blotted it by pressing their lips to the mirrors, leaving dozens of little lip prints. The principal decided something had to be done, so she called the girls to the bathroom and met them there with the custodian.

She explained lip prints caused a major problem for the custodian, who had to clean the mirrors every day. To demonstrate how difficult it was, she asked the custodian to clean one of the mirrors. He took out a long-handled brush, dipped it into the toilet, and scrubbed the mirror. Since then there have been no lip prints on the bathroom mirrors in that middle school. (7)

If we could understand the effect that compromise and toying with the sins of the world has on us, then we would terminate it as quickly as the girls did kissing the mirror. **When you kiss up to sin, you suffer contamination.**

I'm afraid the "Glorious Church" has been derailed. We have compromised our testimony. We have corrupted our influence. We have been confused, constrained, condescended, and contaminated. We have lost our power with God and with man. We are unable to declare the Gospel with demonstration and power like Paul. (I Corinthians 2:4) Something is missing and it's not God's fault. We are at fault, and we need to find out what's wrong and correct the problem.

Today we have more money, more music, more equipment, more people, more knowledge, more methods, and less of God than at any other time in church history. The early church had little money, unimpressive music, practically no equipment, very few people, and lacked in knowledge and wanted for methods. But, they had the power of God. That made all the difference! Until we return to God and experience a full measure of His power in our efforts, we will continue to produce fruitless works that will have little effect on a lost and dying world.

When it comes to pageantry, we are proficient. When it comes to the power, we are pathetic. We have gotten off the track. We have been derailed. We have so much capability in ourselves that we seldom need to reach out and depend on the supernatural intervention of God. Paul describes this as *"having a form of godliness but denying the power."* II Timothy 3:5

I am afraid we are too quick to relegate this scripture to some other faulty, pretentious, and modernistic groups whom we accuse of being far afield of the truth. There is an application here that Evangelical Christians need to own up to.

The word "power" that Timothy uses is the familiar Greek word "dunamis." It means supernatural strength or ability, miraculous power. The word "deny" means to contradict, disavow, reject, and abnegate. The word "abnegate" is an interesting word. It means to give up rights or claims, to renounce. In short, it is saying, "I just don't need that power."

Let's admit it, Evangelical Friend, we have so much of our man-made achievements to rely on that we are not serious candidates for the soul purging, lifestrengthening, ability imparting, or miraculous power of the Holy Spirit in our lives today.

I thank God for all the wonderful accomplishments we have to rejoice over. Our abilities are God given, and we need to use them. Our problem is that when we see what we are accomplishing, we are quick to take the credit and forget that it all comes from God.

God warns His people in Deuteronomy:

> *"So it shall be, when the Lord your God brings you into the land of which He swore to your fathers, to Abraham, Isaac, and Jacob, to give you large and beautiful cities which you did not build, houses full of all good things, which you did not fill, hewn-out wells which you did not dig, vineyards and olive trees which you did not plant – when you have eaten and are full – then beware, lest you forget the Lord who brought you out of the land of Egypt, from the house of bondage."*
>   Deuteronomy 6:10-12

It is not that we have forsaken God, it is just that we have forgotten Him. Not forgotten in the sense of obliterating Him from our minds, but forgotten in the sense of not needing Him to accomplish the work we are doing. We depend more on the arm of human flesh than we do the everlasting arms of God.

Eugene Peterson's edition, **"THE MESSAGE,"** paraphrases Jeremiah 10:23 to show us how dependant we are upon God.

> *"I know, God, that mere mortals can't run their own lives,*
> *that men and women don't have what it takes to take*
> *charge of life. So correct us, God, as you see best."*

Jeremiah had it right! He says we don't know how to run our own lives, but since we will make a futile attempt, he tells God to correct us. When we try to take things into our own hands, we make a mess of things. God has to take corrective measures to get us back on track.

I think we are too accustomed to having church without God. We go through the motions and perform the practices and go away saying, "We had church." Having church is open to semantic opinion. Some interpret having church as being an exercise in emotional calisthenics. Others interpret having church as being a repetition of liturgical practice. Still others interpret having church as taking an hour out of their busy schedule where they occasionally appear in a church building and then disappear like a magician.

This is not an attempt to convince you that my interpretation of having church is to be followed and practiced by everyone. It is an attempt to answer the question **"Do we truly meet God when we go to church?"**

There was a man by the name of Bill whom I came to know and befriend in one of my pastorates. Bill attended what I considered to be a dead, dry, lifeless, modernistic church. I was acquainted with his pastor from clergy meetings we had attended and considered him to be the cause of the dead, dry, lifeless church.

I asked Bill one day,

"How can you attend such a lifeless church? Surely there is nothing there for a man with your spiritual experience to benefit."

Down deep I was hoping Bill would get real spiritual and come to my church. (Lord, forgive me for those carnal cogitations.) Bill looked at me and replied,

"Bob, I meet God every time I go to church. It may be in a hymn we sing; it may be in a scripture that is read; and, wonders of wonders, it may be in something the pastor says in his book report."

(Lord forgive me again for my judgmental attitude that dictates that people meet God by my interpretation of having church.)

There are some requirements for us to meet if we plan to meet God in church. First, you have to come with an open heart. That means you leave behind your preconceived notions about what you think you need and open your heart to what God may have in mind for you. It's important also that you leave your cares and worries outside the church, and worship with an uncluttered and disciplined mind. Often we carry so much baggage into church we have no room to receive anything from the Lord, so that we can leave with something that will benefit us and the world around us.

Another thing that should be left out of church is a critical attitude. Like Dale Carnegie has said, *"Any fool can criticize, condemn, and complain… and most of them do."* (5) It would also help if we prayed before, and we entered the church already built up in the Spirit. We usually go to church looking for something to happen to meet our need and forget that we can be a blessing as well as receive a blessing. When we give out, God gives back good measure, pressed down, shaken together and running over. God is no man's debtor.

We had a saying we often used when I was a young Christian, "When you go to church make sure your cup is right side up." We took this to mean that when you went to church, with the right attitude, for the right purpose, and with expecting faith, you would always meet God and receive what you needed.

To be derailed means to be detached, displaced, and disconnected from the rail on which one travels to a predetermined destination. The church has been derailed and is rambling in so many different directions that they are all thinking they are the ones on the right tract.

Paul warned Timothy that this would happen. *"Now the Spirit expressly says that in latter times some will depart from the faith..."* I Timothy 4:1 This means they were on track once but they were disconnected from *"the faith once delivered to the saints."* Jude 3 We may not go as far astray as those described in Jude 3, but we have been derailed from the practice and procedures of the early church. It is time to **wake up and get back on track to be ready** "without spot or wrinkle" for the coming of the Lord.

Fading Affection
Chapter 2

"But you walked away from your first love - Why? What's going on with you anyway? Do you have any idea how far you've fallen? A Lucifer fall! Turn back! Recover your dear early love. No time to waste, for I'm well on my way to removing your light from the golden circle?"
Revelation 2:4-5 (MSG)

During the reign of Cyrus, (424-401 B.C.) King of Persia, there was a rebel chieftain, Cagular, who constantly harassed the Persian armies. Exasperated by the havoc Cagular created, Cyrus dispatched his forces to capture this autonomous warrior so he could eliminate the problem. Not only would he kill Cagular, but his family as well. When the mighty Cagular arrived, Cyrus rethought his plans. While standing face to face in the throne room, the powerful king asked:

"Cagular, if I were to save your life, what would you do?"

Cagular replied, *"King, I would serve you the rest of my days."*

Cyrus pondered this response, then asked.

"What would you do if I spared the life of your wife?"

Cagular declared, *"Your Majesty, if you spared my wife, I would die for you."*

Upon further reflection, Cyrus not only decided to pardon this condemned soldier, but he made an alliance with Cagular and put him in charge of his troops along the southern border.

As Cagular returned home with his family, he began to talk of the amazing wealth in Cyrus' court. He turned to his wife and asked, ***"Did you see all of the marble? The soldier's armor of silver was magnificent, and what about the solid gold throne that Cyrus sat on?"***

His wife replied, ***"I didn't see any of that."***

In dumbfounded surprise, Cagular asked. *"What did you see?"*

She said, *"I saw only the face of the man who said he would die for me."* (5)

Love and devotion of this magnitude is what we should have for God.

The Apostle Peter thought he had this kind of love for Jesus. When Jesus began to tell the disciples that they would be offended because of Him and would all scatter and leave Him, Peter quickly replied,

"Even if I have to die with You, I will not deny You."

Matthew 26:35

Peter found that his love was deficient, and he ended up denying the lord three times before the next morning. His heart was in the right place, and he was sincere when he made the promise. **It is much easier to promise love than it is to perform love** – we all have demonstrated this fact.

The church in Ephesus left their first love. (Revelation 2:4) Although John had many commendations about the good things this church was doing, he tells those in Ephesus that they had fallen and needed to repent.

I don't see that they had fallen into any particular sin, but John tells them they had fallen from the heights. They must have loved the Lord dearly at one time. They must have had a passion for God that motivated their every act of service. Somewhere along the way, their affection faded, their passion paled, and their love languished. To the Lord, this was serious enough to inspire John to remind them that they had to repent because of this lack of love.

Why would this fading affection be so serious? Why would John have to write that they had to repent for this? What would this loss of love do to them that would require immediate action? The answer: Because **love is the foundation of our relations to God.** John instructs us,

"We love Him because He first loved us."

I John 4:19

Jesus implemented the love relationship when He gave His life for us on the cross at Calvary.

Mel Gibson's film, **THE PASSION OF THE CHRIST**, gives a moving and graphic picture of the agony Christ went through to demonstrate His love for us. As I viewed this film, I found myself thinking maybe the title should have been, **THE PASSION OF THE ENEMIES OF CHRIST**. They seemed driven in their relentless pursuit to inflict such pain upon Him. The real passion, however, was exhibited by the love it took for Christ to endure that pain for lost humanity.

> *"Greater love has no one than this, than to*
> *lay down one's life for his friends."*
>
> John 15:13

A mediocre love would never hold Christ to the cross until His life ebbed away. It would take a passionate love that would cause Him to look beyond the suffering to the completed purpose: redeemed man. We read in Hebrews 12:2,

> *"Looking unto Jesus, the author and finisher of our faith, who for*
> *the joy that was set before Him endured the cross, despising the*
> *shame, and has sat down at the right hand of the throne of God."*

As we receive the overwhelming love of Christ portrayed in the PASSION OF THE CHRIST, should we not strive to return our love to Him with a "Passion for Christ?"

Can Jesus Christ be asking for anything less than a passionate love when He calls us to:

> *"Love one another as I have loved you?"*
>
> John 15:12

This instruction is reinforced when we come to I John 3:16 which says,

> "By this we know love, because He laid down His life for us. And we also ought to lay down our lives for the brethren."

This verse reminds us again,

> "Greater love has no one than this, than to
> lay down one's life for His friends."
>
> John 15:13

Jesus didn't ask us to love Him until He demonstrated his love for us. Jesus said,

> "If you love me, you will obey what I command."
>
> John 14:15 (NIV)

He could look forward and expect us to love Him because He demonstrated love to us. He knew if we really loved Him, keeping His commandments would be no problem.

People often have the mistaken idea that the primary concern for a Christian is to keep the commandments of God. Jesus knew in order for us to keep His commandments faithfully, we would have to love Him. Love would be our motivational force. If our love for Him became faulty, then failing to keep His commandments would become a natural consequence. This would mean the primary need for each Christian would be to keep the love relationship fresh and alive at all times.

What God saw in the church at Ephesus was a serious lessening in their love that would lead to careless living. **Loss of love is the first sign of backsliding or of losing ground**. What God saw in the Ephesians was not the immediate effect of their loss of love, but the eventual effect because they would lose their motivational force to keep His commandments.

Having a persuasion of the redeeming grace of Christ should become the primary concern of every Christian. Each of us must have a convincing testimony of honesty and uprightness before an on-looking world. Trust and justice must be our motto, and love and harmony our earnest pursuit if we are going to have a strong, vital, growing love relationship with the Lord and be ready for His coming.

It is not unreasonable to say we should have a passion for Christ. A passion is a powerful emotion, a strong appetite, a driving fervor or zeal. Without this kind of love for God, we will fall to the affections of the world around us. John had to instruct his children in the Lord.

> *"Do not love the world or the things in the world. If anyone loves the world, the love of the Father is not in him."*
>
> I John 2:15

If we don't have a passion for God, the love of the world will crowd Him out.

The Apostle Paul was a man of passion. He was passionate during the time he served Satan persecuting the Church. And, after his conversion, he served God with the same passion. God used Paul's passion to persuade people. His persuasive passion is described for us in his own words:

> *"Knowing, therefore, the terror of the Lord, we persuade men."*
>
> II Corinthians 5:11.

In Acts, we read an account of Paul's persuasive maneuvers:

> *"And he reasoned in the synagogue every Sabbath, and persuaded both Jews and Greeks."*
>
> Acts 18:4

> *"...the Jews with one accord rose up against Paul and brought him to the judgment seat, saying, This fellow persuades men to worship God contrary to the law."*
>
> Acts 18:12-13

> *"... this Paul has persuaded and turned away many people, saying that they are not gods which are made with hands."*
>
> Acts 19:26

Even in Paul's final days, while he was in chains in Rome, he continued to persuade people.

> "So when they had appointed him a day, many came to him at his lodging, to whom he explained and solemnly testified of the kingdom of God, persuading them concerning Jesus from both the Law of Moses and the Prophets, from morning till evening."
>
> Acts 28:23

Paul didn't try to merely inform people, he was compelled to persuade them. This takes passion. If our love doesn't reach a passion level, we will be among those whose:

> "…love shall wax cold because iniquity shall abound."
>
> Matthew 24:12 (KJV)

Jesus made it clear how important having a strong love relationship with Him would be when He said,

> "You shall love the Lord your God with all your heart, with all your soul, and with all your mind. This is the first and great commandment. And the second is like it: You shall love your neighbor as yourself. On these two commandments hang all the Law and the Prophets."
>
> Matthew 22:37-40

In other words, the foundation on which the Law and the Prophets depends is love and the intensity of this love is "all" of our love.

We are told in Ephesians 4:30,

> "And do not grieve the Holy Spirit of God…"

Of course, we grieve the Holy Spirit when we rebel against God and fail to obey His will for us. The Holy Spirit is capable of being grieved because of His abounding love for us. If we had a measure of this love in our hearts for God, we would be sorrowful about grieving the Holy Spirit and would take measures to correct the problem. Therefore, any tendency to sin is a lack of love for God on our part. People who live loose lives in questionable practices do not love the Lord enough to feel the grief He feels from these acts.

The Holy Spirit is the merging force that assembles our love and directs it toward God.

> *"... the love of God has poured out in our hearts by the Holy Spirit who was given to us."*
>
> Romans 5:5

The Holy Spirit must intensify our capacity to love God if we are to be the Glorious Church that God designed us to be.

Joan Mills, a mother of an affectionate young boy, enjoyed a nightly bedtime ritual with her son, Andy. They each compared how much they loved each other. She would say, *"I wouldn't trade you for all the boys in the world."*

Then he would respond with something like, *"I wouldn't trade you for forty motorcycles,"* or *"I wouldn't trade you for Aunt Judi's pool if it were filled with cash, and I was swimming in it."*

Joan says one comparison has stood out above all others. One time little Andy said, *"I love you with all the pieces of my heart."* (5)

Are there not times when our hearts are scattered like pieces of a puzzle? We are like a confused lover who loves them all but is not ready to commit to anyone. We have to put the pieces of our heart together and

> *"set our affections on things above."*
>
> Colossians 3:2 (KJV)

Then we can say, *"I love you Lord with all the pieces of my heart."* When the pieces of our love for God come together, we will have the heart of God to pray prayers with the passion of God. **We need more passion in our prayers.** The Bible admonishes us to pray such prayers. James tell us,

> *"....the effectual fervent prayer of a righteous man availeth much."*
>
> James 5:16 (KJV)

We are also reminded,

"... He is a rewarder of those who diligently seek Him,"
Hebrews 11:6

"And you will seek Me and find Me, when you search for Me with all your heart."
Jeremiah 29:13

John Bunyan, the writer of **"PILGRIM'S PROGRESS"** encouraged passionate prayer when he said, *"In prayer, it is better to have a heart without words than words without prayer"*

Concerning prayer, C.H. Spurgeon, a prominent writer of religious books said, *"Prayer pulls the rope down below and the great bell rings above in the ears of God. He who communicates with heaven is the man who grasps the rope boldly and pulls continuously with all his might."*

And John Knox, the Scottish preacher who founded the Presbyterian Church, prayed a passionate prayer when he cried, *"Give me Scotland or I die."*

Jesus prayed passionate prayers:

"During the days of Jesus' life on earth, He offered up prayers and petitions with loud cries and tears."
Hebrews 5:7 (NIV)

Paul prayed passionate prayers:

"For I could wish that I myself were cursed and cut off from Christ for the sake of my brothers, those of my own race, the people of Israel."
Romans 9:3 (NIV)

Moses prayed passionate prayers:

"...please forgive their sin – But if not, then blot me out of the book you have written."
Exodus 32:32 (NIV)

This sounds far removed from our brand of bland, dispassionate, generic prayers that come from our calm, cool, and complacent hearts. **We must perform our ministry for Christ with passion.** This means that we will love the lost with a caring heart that drives us to share the good news of the Gospel with them. It also means that we may have to inconvenience ourselves in order to serve others. And, if we believe that Jesus Christ is coming back soon for those who are looking for Him, it will mean that we will be attending the House of God with accelerated frequency, and worship the Lord with a fervent devotion.

After Paul reminds us that,

"We must all appear before the judgment seat of Christ..."
II Corinthians 5:10,

he goes on to say,

"It's no light thing to know that we'll all one day stand in that place of Judgment. That's why we work urgently with everyone we meet to get them ready to face God. God alone knows how well we do this, but I hope you realize how much and deeply we care. We're not saying this to make ourselves look good to you. We just thought it would make you feel good, proud even, that we're on your side and not just nice to your face as so many people are. If I acted crazy, I did it for God, if I acted overly serious, I did it for you. Christ's love has moved me to such extremes. His love has the first and last word in everything we do."
II Corinthians 5:11-14 (Msg)

Repeatedly the Bible instructs us to be passionate in our work:

"Lazy hands make a man poor, but diligent hand bring wealth."
Proverbs 10:4 (NIV)

"A curse on him who is lax in doing the Lord's work."
Jeremiah 48:10 (NIV)

"Whatever your hand finds to do, do it with all your might."
Ecclesiastes 9:10 (NIV)

"Since everything here today might well be gone tomorrow, do you see how essential it is to live a holy life? Daily expect the Day of God, eager for its arrival. The galaxies will burn up and the elements melt down that day – but we'll hardly notice. We'll be looking the other way, ready for the promised new earth, all landscaped with righteousness. So, my dear friends, since this is what you have to look forward to, do your very best to be found living at your best, in purity and peace."
II Peter 3:11-14 (Msg)

In the last passage, Peter is urging us to do our best in the light of what is ahead for us.

Doing our best requires passion. If we fail to reach out for a passionate relationship with God, we will end up with a passive performance in the totality of our lives. Passivity is not just dormant, it is destructive.

On May 25, 1998, Michael Fortier was sentenced to 12 years in prison for being passive. Fortier was the key witness whose testimony helped convict Timothy McVeigh and Terry Nichols in the Oklahoma City bombing. Fortier knew about the extensive plans of his two former Army buddies, but failed to warn the authorities. In a courtroom adjacent to where the Alfred P. Murrah Federal Building once stood, Fortier begged for the forgiveness of those who had lost loved ones. This act of terrorism claimed 168 lives including 19 children, and 500 others were injured on that morning of April 19, 1995.

Upon reflection, Fortier said, *"**I thought his** (McVeigh's) **plan would never bear fruit. I was terribly wrong.**"* He went on to describe his desire for things to be different: *"**I sometimes daydream that I told the police, and I became a hero. But in reality, I'm not.**"* The courtroom's judgment on Fortier's passivity should speak to our tendencies toward spiritual passivity (5).

Our tendency to indifference is not an overnight procedure. It is a gradual occurrence. It is like the various stages of the cooling of an object that is very hot. First it is very, very hot. Then it is very hot. Next it is just hot. It cools down to pretty hot, then it is not so hot. Then it becomes quite warm, and next it cools to lukewarm, and finally it becomes stone cold.

At the beginning, the cooling process is so slight, one would not even notice it. As it moves through the different stages, the change is not radical enough to call attention; therefore, it goes undetected and continues through the stages.

Often spiritual cooling off is undetected until it has gone too far. This was the problem with the church of the Laodiceans. Their love had cooled down to the lukewarm stage, and they weren't even aware of it. In fact, they felt they had need of nothing. (Revelation 3:14-17) If you were to have visited this church, you would probably have said, *"Wow, what a church, they have everything. Let's pattern our church after this one."* They appeared to have it all, but they lacked what they needed most: a passionate love for God.

My wife, Virginia, turned to me recently and said, *"I know now why the Bible says, 'And let us not be weary in well doing; for in due season we shall reap, if we faint not.'* Galatians 6:9 (KJV) *The older I become, the harder it is for me to find inspiration to do certain things."*

The truth is, things for which we have no passion one day will lose their attraction and dwindle from our interests. We will find it harder and harder to maintain a continuing interest in these things. This is particularly true of things in the spiritual realm. Prayer becomes a drag; reading the Word becomes perfunctory; attending church falls into a routine and witnessing is out of the question. What's wrong? We have lost our first love. We have cooled down to lukewarm. And, **we have traded passion for passivity.**

Caught in the Current

Chapter 3

"As Solomon grew old, his wives turned his heart after other gods, and his heart was not fully devoted to the Lord his God, as the heart of David his father had been."

I Kings 11:4 (NIV)

While I was attending Bible School in Green Lane, Pennsylvania, two friends and I decided to take a ride down the Perkiomen River in an inflatable boat. The river was at flood stage, so we had a good swift current to propel us. We had the thrill of shooting the rapids at several spots where the river narrowed and the water became more violent. After several hours into our recreational excursion, I decided I wanted to stop and head back to campus where my girlfriend was waiting for me.

The others agreed, so we looked for a spot on the bank where we could disembark. The river however, had other things in mind. We couldn't get close enough to the bank to grab anything that might help stop us. Finally we spotted a fallen tree trunk lying in the river. We thought this could provide ample opportunity for us to ram it with our rubber boat and enable us to get off and walk along the tree trunk to the riverbank.

The current was too strong. As soon as we hit the tree trunk, the boat capsized and the current pulled us under and swept us on down the river. The situation became increasingly serious as the current literally pinned us against the submerged tree trunks that had fallen into the river. We had to struggle to untangle ourselves from the submerged trees, and again be swept away only to be pinned against another tree.

In the terrifying process we were separated and it became a matter of "every man for himself." I don't know about the other fellows, but I knew I did some praying in between tree trunks and submersion struggles. Finally – no doubt due to my Jonah prayers – we came to a spot in the river where there were no sunken tree trunks, and we all made it safely to the riverbank. I came away from that experience with the awareness of how helpless one is when he is "caught in the current."

When Adam and Eve disobeyed God and partook of the forbidden fruit, they initiated the flow of the current of fleshly desire. Their son, Cain, was caught in that current and, in a jealous rage, he killed his brother, Abel. **Adam and Eve experienced a small sample of the ruinous effect their sin had on humanity.**

As time passed, this current only increased in strength until,

"The Lord saw how great man's wickedness on earth had become and that every inclination of the thoughts of his heart was only evil all the time."

Genesis 6:5 (NIV)

God interrupted man's depravity by sending a flood that destroyed all mankind except the remaining seven persons on the ark with Noah.

The reprieve God gave during Noah's day was short-lived. Soon men rebelled again as they sought to build a tower to reach into the heavens. God saw that this rebellion was a unanimous effort and would affect everyone on earth. For this reason, God confused their language so that they could not communicate and therefore, they had to discontinue their project. This forced the people to scatter throughout the earth fulfilling God's command to Noah after the flood to:

"…*be fruitful and multiply, and fill the earth*

Genesis 9:1

God continued to deal with man by raising up the nation of Israel through Abraham. Through Israel, God would reveal His commandments, laws, principles, and instructions for right living. These instructions proved to be more than man could fulfill in his human effort, so God provided forgiveness for man's transgressions through animal sacrifice. The purpose for these sacrifices for sin was completed when God sent His Son, Jesus Christ, to die on the cross for the sins of the world. (John 3:16)

God knew that man needed help to live a life of victory over sin, so He sent the Holy Spirit. Paul explained:

> *"For the law of the Spirit of life in Christ Jesus has made me free from the law of sin and death. For what the law could not do in that it was weak through the flesh, God did by sending His own Son in the likeness of sinful flesh, on account of sin. He condemned sin in the flesh, that the righteous requirements of the law might be fulfilled in us who do not walk according to the flesh, but according to the Spirit."*
>
> Romans 8:2

We, therefore, can be either "Spirit" driven or "flesh" driven.

Wouldn't it be nice if we could say at this point, "And we all lived happily ever after?" The truth is the battle goes on. We have the provisions to overcome the flesh, but we have to implement these on a continuing basis.

Scripture makes it clear that **there is a battle going on between the flesh and the Spirit:**

> *"For the flesh lusts against the Spirit, and the Spirit lusts against the flesh, and these are contrary to one another, so that you do not do the things that you wish."*
>
> Galatians 5:17

The word "lusts" here means to desire deeply, to long for, to set the heart upon. The word "contrary" from this same scripture means to have extreme dislike, to be adverse to, to have repugnance for. As you can see, these two words are exact opposites, pulling in two different directions.

What makes this battle between the sinful flesh and the Holy Spirit such a contrary battle is that it is a spiritual war. The sinful flesh and the Holy Spirit are diametrically opposed and are counter to, hostile toward, and antagonistic against each other.

I THINK WE ALL ARE VERY MUCH AWARE THAT THE FLESH LUSTS, DESIRES DEEPLY, LONGS FOR, AND SETS ITS HEART ON THINGS THAT ARE AGAINST THE THINGS OF THE SPIRIT.

This means God sets His heart on things for us that are far above anything the flesh could ever fulfill. If we could see things in their true perspective, and what Gods plans will produce when they are fulfilled, we would have no problem following God's ways. Our big problem is that the flesh obscures our vision and contaminates our understanding, and we find it easier to drift with the current of our inclinations and repel the pull of the Spirit.

There is a thrill, a surge, a rush in committing sin. If there were no pleasure in sin, there would be no temptation to it. Can you imagine the excitement Eve experienced as she considered the possibilities of the forbidden fruit? She would feel the surge of discovery and enter into the mysteries of the knowledge of God. She would have the knowledge of good and evil, just like God.

What made this experience even more irresistible was that it was a "forbidden fruit." Proverbs 9:17 concedes that: *"Stolen waters are sweet."*

Put a sign on a newly seeded lawn. "STAY OFF THE GRASS," and see what happens. For some, it's an invitation.

Once during the holidays before his conversion, early church father, Augustine, robbed a pear tree. He tells of the event with extraordinary profundity. He desired to rob the tree, and he did rob it. But, he was not impelled by either hunger or poverty. In fact, he did not want the pears at all. There were better ones in his own orchard. Even after the theft, he took no joy in what he had stolen. *"But I took joy,"* he says, *"in the theft and the sin."* (7)

James declares,

> "But every man is tempted, when he is drawn
> away from his own lust, and enticed."
>
> James 1:14 (KJV)

To be "drawn away" means to drag forth, and it shows the powerful pull temptation has on us. In ancient times, a conquering army would parade the defeated captives through the streets, at times, dragging them and humiliating them to show they had overpowered and conquered this vanquished people.

This is what happens when a person is being invaded by temptation, dragged down and humiliated by a captivating power. It's like being caught in the current of a river and not knowing where it will end.

A pastor warned his handsome new assistant about the dangers of immorality in the ministry. The assistant said that he always did his socializing in a group setting and concluded that *"there is safety in numbers."* The wise pastor replied, **"Yes, that is so, but there is more safety in Exodus."** (3)

This must be what Paul had in mind when he instructed his young assistant Timothy:

"Flee also youthful lusts, but persue righteousness, faith, love, peace…"
II Timothy 2:22

Take note that Paul instructed Timothy to flee, run away, and avoid youthful lusts because of their power to drag him down to humiliation. But he also tells him he must pursue righteousness, faith, love, and peace. One does not have to pursue sin, it is an inborn component of our fallen nature. On the other hand, when we are born again, we

"…put off the old man with his deeds, and have put on the new man, who is renewed in knowledge according to the image of him who created him."
Colossians 3:9-10

This living after the new man has to be pursued, sought after, and desired, or the old man will come back to life and resume his battle to drag us down into a sinful lifestyle.

The wonderful thing about putting off the old man and putting on the new man is that **we have help from God to live the new life, through the new man.** The Holy Spirit lusts (desires deeply, longs for, and sets His heart upon) the things that are against the flesh as much as the flesh lusts against the Holy Spirit. In other words, we have a current pulling us against the tendencies of the sinful flesh. It is up to us to

> "...yield ourselves unto God, as those that are alive from the dead, and our members as instruments of righteous unto God."
>
> Romans 6:13 (KJV)

Yielding to God is the determining factor as to who will win the battle of the flesh and the Spirit.

Billy Graham once said, *"The devil will always have a ship ready when a man wants to sail away from God."* This is so very true, but the devil can't make us board it, only we on our own volition can board this ship.

Society today is no friend of the Spirit. Sinful man is in alliance with the immoral trend of the fleshly pull. We can see an ever-increasing current that is pulling us down toward the lusts of the flesh. Paul indicated this would be true when he wrote,

> "But evil men and seducers shall wax worse and worse, deceiving and being deceived,"
>
> II Timothy 3:13 (KJV)

We may wonder, "how can morals become any worse?" But somehow they do.

Statistics compiled in 2003 by the Barna Group of Ventura, California reveal a decaying trend in the moral values of American society today. The Barna Group interviewed, via telephone, a random nationwide sample of 1,024 adults to determine what was morally acceptable. The group was divided into five different groups: all adults, evangelicals, those born again, other faiths, and atheists/agnostics. A sample of the poll revealed that 60% of all adults, 12% of evangelicals, 49% of those born again, 70% of other faiths, and 87% of atheists/agnostics believe that living with someone of the opposite sex without being married is morally acceptable.

I am not surprised that 87% of those who are atheist/agnostic believe that this is morally acceptable. They have no moral guidelines to inspire them. I am surprised that 12% of evangelicals (the cream of the church crop) and 49% of those claiming to be born again, believe this is morally acceptable.

A further revelation was uncovered when the Barna Group computed the response to this question, as it was viewed from a generational perspective. Their findings showed that 75% of Mosaics (those born between 1984 and 2002); 67% of Busters (those born between 1965 and 1983); 60% of Boomers (those born between 1946 and 1964), and 51% of elders (also called builders/seniors, born between 1927 and 1945), believed that living with someone of the opposite sex without being married, was morally acceptable. (8)

One can easily see from these findings that **each successive generation was more permissive in their interpretation of morality.** In a Basic Youth Conflict Seminar, Bill Gothard said, "What the parents do in moderation, the children do in excess." When you consider this in light of moral values today, you recognize that we are on a fast train to destruction.

George Barna further stated: "Most of the people we interviewed believe that they are highly moral individuals and identify other people as responsible for the nation's moral decline. Yet, deep inside, they sense that something is wrong in our society. They simply have not been able to put two and two together to recognize their personal liability regarding the moral condition of our nation." (8)

It is a soul-searching time for every one of us. We must ask ourselves. "What am I doing to contribute to the trend of moral decay?" and "What am I doing to correct this condition?" **Until we become a part of the solution, we will be a part of the problem.**

Even the spiritual appetites of modern-day Christians are caught in the pull of the sinful influences surrounding them. Paul warned Timothy:

> *"You're going to find that there will be times when people will have no stomach for solid teaching, but will fill up on spiritual junk food – catchy opinions that tickle their fancy. They'll turn their backs on truth and chase mirages. But you – keep your eye on what you're doing, accept the hard times along with the good, keep the Message alive, do a thorough job as God's servant."*
> II Timothy 4: 3-5 (Msg)

If you have any spiritual observations concerning what's happening in the church world today, you are painfully aware that the message of II Timothy 4:3-5 is taking place right before your eyes!

In a classic leadership cartoon by Mary Chambers, two couples are seated in a living room engaged in a Bible study. One of the women is speaking.

"Well," she says. *"I haven't actually died to sin, but I did feel kind of faint once."*(7)

We can't very well overcome sin if we don't die to it by putting the old man to death. Instructions for crucifying the old man are given in Romans 6. Water baptism is an illustration of what happens to us in a spiritual sense.

"Therefore we were buried with Him through baptism unto death, that just as Christ was raised from the dead by the glory of the Father, even so we also should walk in newness of life."

Romans 6:4

When we are buried, we are dead. If we weren't dead before we were buried, we will be after we are buried. The illustration continues as we are raised up from the waters of baptism. We are spiritually raised up to walk in newness of life. Paul continues with his instructions:

"Likewise you also reckon yourselves to be dead indeed to sin, but alive to God in Christ Jesus our Lord."

Romans 6:11

The word "reckon" means to take an inventory, to make a computation, to come to a conclusion. What Paul is saying is - "Since you understand that you are dead to sin, like a person buried in water, and are raised up to newness of life, as Christ was raised up in His resurrection, now you must reckon (take inventory, make a computation, come to the conclusion) that this is a fact in your everyday Christian living."

People are inclined to drift away from the things to which they fail to give earnest heed. We see it in marriages, couples who drift farther and farther apart because they fail to give attention to their relationship.

We see it in our memories. We begin to lose our recall capabilities with things we fail to rehearse regularly.

We see this in our acquired capabilities, such as playing a musical instrument. If we haven't kept in practice, we will hit some sour notes or mess up our timing in strategic places. Our spiritual lives are not unlike our natural lives. We tend to drift away from spiritual things if we do not keep them vital to our hearts. This is especially true because of the current of declining morals.

We are told to:

"Give the more earnest heed to the things we have heard, lest we drift away."

Hebrews 2:1

The word "earnest" means, more superabundantly, more exceedingly, or more frequently. It is a picture of how diligent we must be to retain what we have learned, so these things do not slip away from us, or we drift away from them.

James was also dealing with this problem when he wrote,

"But be doers of the word, and not hearers only, deceiving yourselves. For if anyone is a hearer of the word and not a doer, he is like a man observing his natural face in a mirror, or he observes himself, goes away, and immediately forgets what kind of man he was. But he who looks into the perfect law of liberty and continues in it, and is not a forgetful hearer but a doer of the work, this one will be blessed in what he does."

James 1:22-25

What happened to the forgetful hearer was that he didn't give earnest heed to the things he heard. He failed to apply and act upon them, and he soon drifted away from them. It goes without saying that he was drifting further from God in his spiritual status.

During the course of Christ's earthly ministry, it became increasingly apparent that there was a current flowing against the ebb and flow of His plan and purpose. Through the deceptive intentions of Satan, the religious leaders were firm in their crusade to silence this popular miracle worker who was undermining their authority.

Their method was mob psychology. It was so evident in Nazareth when Jesus spoke soul-searching truth to the people that convicted their self-serving behavior. The current of their anger flowed so vigorously that they sought to throw Him off a cliff. He passed through the midst of them and went on his way. (Luke 4:23-30)

This mob psychology surfaced again when He declared:

"My Father loves Me, because I lay down
My life that I may take it again."

John 10:17

Many, realizing He claimed equality with God, responded by accusing Him of having a demon, and they again attempted to seize Him. (John 10:18-39)

This power of human behavior seems to have spewed out as Jesus is hanging on the cross, and the crowd is launching insults at Him. They jeered:

"You who destroy the temple and build it in three days, save
Yourself, and come down from the cross. Likewise the chief priests
also, mocking among themselves with the scribes, said, 'He saved
others, Himself He cannot save. Let the Christ, the King of
Israel, descend now from the cross that we may see and believe.'
Even those who were crucified with Him reviled Him."

Mark 15:29-32

Paul offers his teaching on what is needed to contend with the powerful current that tends to sweep us away:

"Finally, my brethren, be strong in the Lord and in the power of
His might. ...take up the whole armor of God, that you may be
able to withstand in the evil day, and having done all, to stand."

Ephesians 6:10, 13

The word "withstand" means to vigorously oppose, to bravely resist, to stand your ground, or to stand face to face against an adversary. It is a picture of the supernatural power that is needed to endure the rushing current of satanic opposition tugging at us perpetually.

Being a Christian isn't for sissies. It takes courage to go against the current. It takes more than a wishy-washy commitment. It will take no less than the surrender Jesus demanded when he said,

> *"If anyone desires to come after Me, Let him deny himself, and take up his cross, and follow Me."*
>
> Matthew 16:24

We are caught in the current and are being swept downstream on an every-increasing speed. **It's time to wake up and return to God.** It is time to get ready!

Facing Our Fall
Chapter 4

"Behold, the Lord's hand is not shortened, that it cannot save, Nor His ear heavy that it cannot hear. But your iniquities have separated you from your God, and your sins have hidden His face from you, so that He will not hear."
Isaiah 59: 1-2

When I was young, I used to enjoy throwing stones in the lake near my home. One particularly calm day, I came to the lake to do my stone throwing and found it to be as smooth as glass. I could see the beautiful reflection of the hill on the opposite shore, displaying its fall colors.

Should I spoil this serene scene with the toss of a stone? I couldn't resist. I flung the first stone I could find into the tranquil setting, and immediately, this beautiful scene was disrupted by distorting waves and raging ripples.

This is a picture of what happened when Adam threw a stone of self-indulgence in to the lake of God's glorious love and tolerance. We refer to this intolerable act as the fall of man. **A fall always takes us down**. We never fall up. A fall always takes us to a lower level. The primary cause for this happening is an effect called gravity. Webster's New World College Dictionary says, *"gravity is a force that tends to draw all bodies into the earth's sphere to the center of the earth."*

When I stub my toe and fall, gravity tends to pull me down until I hit bottom, and usually it is with a jarring effect.

Sin is like gravity in that it pulls us down to a lower level. It is a power that drags, tugs, and hauls us down under its control and influence. It begins with a desirable attraction and ends with a destructive distraction.

Salvation is the power of God that brings us up out of our fallen condition and starts us going in the right direction, as David instructs us in Psalms 40:4 (KJV),

> *"He brought me up also out of an horrible pit, out of the miry clay, and set my feet upon a rock, and established my goings."*

Paul reminds us in Ephesians 2:6 that we are raised up together, and made to sit together in heavenly places in Christ Jesus.

> *"Sitting together in heavenly places" is a permanent position founded upon and conditional to our association with Christ in His resurrection.*

> *"Therefore we were buried with Him through baptism into death, that just as Christ was raised from the dead by the glory of the father, even so we also should walk in newness of life. For if we have been united together in the likeness of His death, certainly we also shall be in the likeness of His resurrection."*
>
> Romans 6:4-5

What a marvelous position we have sitting together with Christ in heavenly places! This means we are sharing His victory over sin, Satan, and servitude. Certainly we will have sufficient fortitude to remain committed to this spectacular relationship. However, given an honest appraisal of the facts as they present themselves to us, we come to realize that many people fall from their privileged position in Christ Jesus. **We have a responsibility, to continue in the faith:**

> *"And you, who once were alienated and enemies in your mind by wicked works, yet now He has reconciled in the body of His flesh through death, to present you holy, and blameless, and above reproach in His sight – if indeed you continue in the faith, grounded and steadfast, and are not moved away from the hope of the gospel which you heard."*
>
> Colossians 1:21-23

The scriptures are cluttered with examples of those who once walked with God but fell flat on their faces in a spiritual collapse. Samson was a servant of God who liked to toy with sin. He repeatedly would amuse himself by skirting the boundaries of self-indulgence, always recoiling to display the flair of his supernatural strength. He began to think his strength was attributable to his own ability. One day he stepped over the line of God's patient tolerance and experienced the fruit of his undisciplined indulgence at the hand of a temptress named Delilah.

In his fall, Samson lost his strength, he lost his eyes, and he lost the patient leniency of his merciful, loving God. What a price to pay for a few moments of fleshly pleasure. Even though Samson regained enough strength to destroy his enemies, he lost his own life in the process. His loss was incomprehensible and the price for restoration (to God) was the ultimate of human sacrifice.

We, like Samson, are inclined to squander our God-given gifts and abilities on self-exalting objectives. Our fall may not be quite so dramatic and costly as his was, but we, nevertheless, fall from our exalted position with Christ and terminate the effectiveness in our battle with the enemy. Can you look back from where you are today and remember better times in your spiritual life? If so, you have fallen.

It may not be that you have turned your back on God, but you have lost something that is vital in your relationship with God. Do you think this is God's will for You? Are you making any plans to return to that place of intimate fellowship with Him? Do you really think you are ready for His coming?

Another colossal fall recorded for us in scripture is that of King Saul. His story starts out with an exhibit of his honest humility. When he (Samuel) sought to proclaim him as their (Israel's) king, Saul was nowhere to be found. (I Samuel 10:17-24) I think the people were pleased that they had a man who was not arrogant and self—promoting. What seemed to have been his strength, however, eventually became his downfall.

Saul's instructions from Samuel were to wait at Gilgal until he, Samuel, arrived to offer a burnt offering to God. When Samuel didn't appear at the appointed time, Saul intruded into the office of the priest and sacrificed the burnt offering. (I Samuel 13:8-10)

This was an insolent act against the command of God. As a result of his failure, Saul was rejected as king. (I Samuel 13:11-15) It would seem that David realized the immensity of the fall of Saul and Jonathan when he sang the "Song of the Bow" including the often repeated phrase,

> *"How the mighty have fallen…"*
> II Samuel 1:17-27

One of the things we learn from Saul's experience is that **we can fall even in the area of our known strength.** "Humble Saul" assumed a position for which he was neither qualified nor commissioned. Pride and arrogance, traits he seemed to have well under control, became the culprits that toppled him.

> *"Therefore let him that thinks he stands take heed lest he fall."*
> I Corinthians 10:12

Paul was referring to those in Old Testament times who were blessed with abundant opportunity to make good, but fell. His warning to us is ***"Don't let this happen to you."***

But this has happened to us in spite of Paul's warning. We have trekked down the same trail that Saul traveled, the trail of unsuspecting self-confidence.

Satan will devise a strategy that is personalized for you. Some people are brought down through weaknesses that he has discovered and takes advantage of. He hits them in that weakness and they fall, sometimes repeatedly. If a plan works, Satan will continue to use it. Some people, however, have overcome their weaknesses to Satan's attack and that area is ineffective. This is when he is apt to march right in and attack us in our strengths. This is the tactic Satan used on Saul, who at first was humble and retiring, but he didn't know how to handle power and authority. A strong area of our lives, unprotected by the power of God, quickly degenerates into a weakness when we fail to rely on God for assistance in our battle. Paul confessed,

> *"When I am weak, then I am strong."*
> II Corinthians 12:9

Weakness compels us to rely on God for our strength, but where we are strong, we tend to rely on our own ability.

The story of King David is a thrilling and riveting account of a man who enjoyed the merciful favor of God. We see him rallying a divided and demoralized nation and bringing them back to unity and vitality. His military accomplishments bring Israel back to national prominence.

Most notable of all of David's achievements; however, is found in the amazing title God gave him:

"A man after God's own heart."

I Samuel 13:14

David would fit into God's prophetic plan and be a testimony of God's dealings to all nations. With this array of glorious accomplishments, it seems demeaning to think of David having a fall. But, the man who sang about King Saul, ***"How the mighty have fallen,"*** himself became the second verse to that song. It was during this era when kings went out to war that David decided to stay home. David sent Joab, the Captain of his army, out to do battle. David, himself, stayed in Jerusalem.

One evening, he took a stroll on the roof of the palace. There, across the way, a bathing beauty, named Bathsheba, presented a temptation to David that he could not resist.

Being king, and knowing that nothing could be withheld from him, David devised a plan to have Bathsheba for his own pleasure.

A short time later, after what would appear to have been a one-night episode, she announced to him that she was with child. David knew that he was in trouble. He had to devise another plan to clear him of public exposure.

His first attempt to conceal his sin was to bring Bathsheba's husband, Uriah, back from battle. This would allow Uriah to sleep with his wife and to conclude that he was the father of the child. But that didn't work. Uriah was too conscientious to sleep with his wife when his war buddies were out risking their lives for their nation.

It became apparent to David that his only option was to get rid of Uriah. He sent a letter to his army captain, Joab, to send Uriah into the hottest part of the battle and to withdraw the troops from him so that he would be slain. This plan worked! David got rid of Uriah, but he didn't get rid of his sin.

How could this man after God's own heart ever think he could get away with such conduct? He was guilty of adultery, lying, dissembling, and murder. This record of ruinous deeds would seem to disqualify David from ever being an instrument of God.

If it depended on perfection for us to be used by God, none of us would make the grade. **God has provided a road to restoration through humility, confession, and repentance.**

David was a man after God's own heart not because he never failed, but because when he failed he was willing to take this road to restoration.

The fall of David reminds us that no matter how blessed we are; no matter how privileged we are; no matter how favored we are, God still expects us to hold to the standards of His Word. It also reminds us that **when we fall, there is hope for restoration, if we are humble and we repent.**

Solomon's fall could be considered more of a compromise. He didn't hit bottom he just fell to a lower level in his relationship with God.

We are informed about it in I Kings 11:4,

"For it was so, when Solomon was old, that his wives turned his heart after other gods, and his heart was not loyal to the Lord his God, as was the heart of his father, David."

It is interesting to note that Solomon's loyalty to God is compared to that of David, his father. We know David had his failures, but this scripture shows us that God considered Solomon's failure to be worse than that of David.

The displeasure of God is seen in that He said He would tear the kingdom from Solomon and give one tribe to Solomon's son, Rehoboam, and the rest of the tribes to Solomon's servant, Jeroboam. This was carried out when Solomon's trusted servant Jeroboam, rebelled against him and drew away the support of many of the disgruntled people.

Furthermore, God raised up Hadad, the Edomite, and Rezon, the son of Eliadah. Both men were adversaries of Solomon all the rest of his life. This was difficult for Solomon to handle since his kingdom had enjoyed peace and safety prior to this. The point to recognize here is that the adversity that Solomon suffered was imposed by God in His displeasure for Solomon's fall. Solomon lost the touch of God on his life and floundered for the rest of his life.

Solomon's failure is the third verse of David's song. *"How the Mighty have fallen."* The song has never stopped being sung, down through the ages. Leaders, and laity alike, are still hitting the skids to carnal indulgence undermining the power and credibility of the church.

Compromise was the culprit that tumbled Solomon to his demise. Many wives caused difficult decisions for him. Each wife came with her baggage of religious relics and demanded equal rights for the god of her persuasion. Solomon's compromise forged an opening for him to support and even participate with his wives in the abominable practices in which they indulged.

> *"For Solomon went after Astoreth, the goddess of the Sidonians, and after Milcom, the abomination of the Ammonites. Solomon did evil in the sight of the Lord, and did not fully follow the Lord, as did his father, David. Then Solomon built a high place for Chemosh, the abomination of Moab, on the hill that is east of Jerusalem, and for Molech, the abomination of the people of Ammon. And he did likewise for all his foreign wives who burned the incense and sacrificed to their gods."*
>
> I Kings 11:5-8

The story of Solomon and his compromising calamity reminds me of an old Russian parable. A big game hunter had a large bear in the cross hairs of his rifle. He was just about to pull the trigger when the bear spoke in a soft, soothing voice. *"Isn't it better to talk than to shoot? What do you want? Let us negotiate the matter."*

Lowering the rifle, the hunter replied. *"I want a fur coat."*

"Good," said the bear, *"that is a negotiable request. I only want a full stomach, so let us negotiate a compromise."*

They sat down to negotiate, and after a time the bear walked away, alone. The negotiations had been successful. The bear had a full stomach, and the hunter had his fur coat. **Compromise rarely satisfies both sides in equal measure.** (3)

Solomon may have started out compromising with his many wives, but when it came down to the final analysis, the wives ended up with the full stomach, and the fur coat. Solomon only reaped the fruit of his foolish compromise. Webster's New World College Dictionary defines "compromise" as "an adjustment of opposing principles by modifying some aspects of each." When you modify the principles of God's Word, you destroy the foundation upon which it is established.

God's Word is His covenant with man and is not negotiable.

"Forever, O Lord, your word is settled in heaven."

Psalm 119:89

"Heaven and earth will pass away, but My words will by no means pass away."

Mark 13:31

When we play with the principles of God, we pervert the premise for a clear concept of right and wrong. We see the confusion of right and wrong in the church today. Church leadership is ready to ordain homosexuals to the ministry, the authenticity of the virgin birth is being questioned, and the certainty of the inerrancy of the Word of God is being undermined. I heard over the radio recently about a minister who said, **"The inerrancy of the scriptures is silly."** If the inerrancy of the scriptures is silly, anyone who would put their trust in the scriptures would be silly. That would include Jesus, the Apostles, Billy Graham, and every evangelical believer who makes a stand for Christ today. How could anyone make such a statement about the scriptures when they are the absolute foundation upon which the plan of God is founded? The only conclusion one can come to is that they have fallen away from the truth.

Peter talked about some untaught and unstable people who twisted the teachings of Paul to their own destruction as they did the rest of the scriptures. His warning to the faithful brethren was, since they had the example of these people they should:

"Beware lest you fall from your own steadfastness, being led away with the error of the wicked."

II Peter 3:14-17

Peter teaches here that not only the unlearned and unstable can twist truth around to their own destruction, but that even the faithful brethren can fall from their own steadfastness. It was to the commendable church at Ephesus that John wrote:

> *"Remember from where you have fallen, repent, and do the first works, or else I will come to you quickly and remove your lamp stand from its place."*
>
> Revelation 2:5

The removal of their lamp stand didn't mean that they would cease to exist, but that the light of their influence would be discontinued.

It's time to exert ourselves to make sure that our light is still shining where we live, and that we do not fall under the influence of the world's standards.

Slipping to Substitutes
Chapter 5

> *"For my people have committed two evils. They have forsaken Me, the fountain of living waters, and hewn themselves cisterns- broken cisterns that can hold no water."*
> JEREMIAH 2:13

On the French Rivera, it was such an important status symbol to have a balcony on an apartment, that today, it is quite common to see a balcony painted on the exterior walls of apartment houses. People even painted wet laundry hanging on a clothesline, just to give it a touch of reality. (3) These wall paintings were a cheap substitute for the real thing. They may have had an appearance of a balcony, but you wouldn't want to step out on one. God's first two commandments make it abundantly clear that He wants our complete loyalty. His instructions read:

> *"You shall have no other gods before Me. You shall not make for yourself a carved image."*
> Exodus 20:3-4

Being devoted to only one God was a practice that would be very different from the other nations around them. Those nations had many gods who were creations of their own fancies.

God will settle for nothing less than total allegiance. He has the right, since we are beings of His creation. If we refuse to submit to Him, we will end up creating a god that will meet our own specifications. This will make us the creator and God our creation. Man, being self-centered and egocentric, will design a god that will bring him pleasure and satisfaction. These are sensations that God seeks to derive from us through our devotion and commitment to Him. God explains the motive of His commands to us by telling us:

> *"For I, the Lord your God, am a jealous God."*
>
> Exodus 20:5

The word "jealous" means to be envious, to provoke even to anger. Jealousy demonstrates the powerful relationship God seeks to build with His people. God doesn't want Satan to seduce His children, and He doesn't want His children flirting with the world. God tells us plainly:

> *"...not to love the world, neither the things that are in the world because if one loves the world, the love of the Father is not in him."*
>
> I John 2:15

We resort to some substitute that will give the impression that we still have the goods, and we will go to any lengths necessary to protect this impression. Nowhere do we see this deception more prevalent than in the church. The church has such outstanding examples to live up to that it finds itself challenged to imitate these patterns. Such as:

> *"Enoch, who was translated without seeing death, because he pleased God; Noah, who built an ark and preserved God's whole creation; Abraham and Sarah, who defied the odds and had a child in their old age; the Children of Israel passing through the Red Sea on dry land; the walls of Jericho falling down as a result of Israel merely marching around the walls at God's command; God delivering Daniel from a lion's den, and David slaying a giant with a sling. On and on the stories go of those who endured cruel mocking and scourging, were imprisoned, stoned, sawn in two, and slain with the sword of whom the world was not worthy..."*
>
> Hebrews 11:1-39

To be numbered among this array of mighty warriors, one would want to have the real thing. But somewhere along the way, it seems the church has lost the reality of God's mighty power, and injected their own substitute to keep up the illusion that all is well. Again, we refer to II Timothy 3:5,

"Having a form of godliness, but denying the power."

The word "form" here means semblance or appearance. In other words, they go through the motions. They have an appearance of godliness, but there is no power there to back it up.

This is such a revealing picture of much of the church in America today. It has "glorious form" but pitiful performance. **We have slipped to substitutes,** thinking we can keep up the semblance and make it seem that all is well. But all is not well! We are far from the glorious church that God desires us to be. We are helplessly mired in the quick sand of spiritual substitutions. We have the form, but where is the power?

When I was a younger man and a bit more dexterous in my physical skills, I met with some of my preacher friends to engage in a friendly game of golf. After my first swing, one of my golfing buddies commented on the good form and style I had when I teed off. I was quite elated when the others all chimed in and agreed.

After about the fifth hole, a lone player came up and asked if he could play through. Realizing we were quite talkative and a bit slow in our progress, we willingly obliged him. He eyed the next hole, which was a dogleg to the left. Then he studied the tall trees that stood between him and the hole. He laid his ball flat on the ground, and without the aid of a tee, he gripped his club like a baseball player grips a bat, and lambasted that ball up over the trees and on to the green.

We all stood there, amazed at the feat of the unorthodox golf ball hacking fanatic. Suddenly it was my turn to show off my form. I teed up the ball as perfectly as I could. I gripped my club, taking care to overlap my thumbs, as every good golfer knows is right. I arched my leg and stiffened my arm and swung with what I was sure was the most beautiful swing I had ever delivered.

My form was perfect. My problem was that I missed the ball. I heard a roar in the background. It was my buddies, not cheering me on, but laughing at my plight. I had great form, but lousy performance. I am afraid the Church in America has all the semblance of a spiritual organization, but it fails to connect with the needs of the world. We swing well- we just don't hit the ball. We look good on paper, but we fail to tally up on the bottom line. We have lost the manifestation of God's power and resorted to too many substitutes.

The major muff of the church is that we have decided our system is better than God's. We call it God's system, but since we have been derailed, we are forced to either repent or devise our own system. We find it much easier to revise than to repent. We are now convinced that our system is better than God's.

Cain thought he had a better plan than God. He decided an offering of his fruit of the ground would be a good sacrifice to offer to God. He brought such an offering and God refused to accept it. Cain's brother, Abel, also brought an offering of his chosen trade, the first born of the flock. God had respect for Abel's offering and accepted it, no doubt by consuming it with fire.

There were at least two reasons why God refused Cain's offering. One reason was because his attitude was wrong.

> *"The sacrifice of the wicked is an abomination to the Lord."*
> Proverbs 15:8

This would prove that God examines the spiritual state of a worshipper. A second reason for God's refusal was that He was in the process of teaching the principle of blood sacrifice in preparation of the redemptive work of Christ on the cross. There is reason to believe that Abel caught this teaching and thus, by faith, offered a more excellent sacrifice than Cain. (Hebrews 11:4.)

God pursues the plight of Cain by telling him:

> *"If you do well, will you not be accepted? And if you do not do well, sin lies at your door.*
> Genesis 4:7

This was lesson time for Cain. God made it very clear that Cain was guilty of sin that needed to be dealt with. If Cain had no previous knowledge of the preference of God, he had all the study material available to teach him. There had to be animals slain to provide skins to cover his mother and father when they had sinned. Right before his eyes, he saw how God accepted the animal sacrifice of his brother, Abel.

His immediate response should have been to purchase an animal from Abel and offer it to God in order to become accepted. The murder of Abel was not just an attack on Abel, it was an attack on God. Cain refused to learn anything from his own personal insight. God may have preferred an animal sacrifice, but Cain had put too much hard work into tilling the soil to let his sacrifice go without respect. The lesson to be learned from Cain is that our way of handling things is not better than God's. If we don't understand His ways, it's lesson time. If we don't study His lesson, it's repentance time. **If we don't repent and change, it's judgment time.**

The kingdom of Judah had lost connection with their God. Isaiah depicts the degenerate conditions they had plunged to:

"How the faithful city has become a harlot! It was full of justice, righteousness lodged in it, but now murderers. Your silver has become dross, your wine mixed with water. Your princes are rebellious, and companions of thieves; everyone loves bribes and follow after rewards. They do not defend the fatherless, nor does the cause of the widow come before them."

Isaiah 1:21-23

These verses show how Judah was at one time, a faithful, just, and righteous people. The analogy quickly changes and depicts them substituting dross for silver. They made watered down wine pass for the full strength. They turned their backs on justice and sought bribes instead. All of this eventually enabled them to murder and think that they could get away with it. They were not unlike Cain who started out with a proud thought, moved to a jealous heart, and finally gave place to an angry spirit that enabled him to murder with a clear conscience.

The nation of Israel decided they wanted a king. They wanted to be like other nations who could glory in their king and revel in his splendor.

God made it known from the start that they had rejected Him and resorted to their self-devised substitute. (I Samuel 8:7)

What would have happened if Israel had remained under God's rule and had followed His leadership? What kind of nation would they have been? Israel would have been very different from the other nations. They would have avoided the disciplinary acts God had to display for their rebellion. The nation would have been a powerful witness to those around them. They would have been regarded as being very special to God, and very unusual to the other nations. The words, "special" and "unusual" are definitions to the word "peculiar" found in Titus 2:14 (KJV).

> *"And, Jesus gave himself for us, that he might redeem us from all iniquity, and purify unto himself a peculiar people, zealous of good works."*

We would rather conform than conflict. We don't like to be different, we want to be like those around us. The price for being different is often more than we want to pay.

I had a personal experience with this in my pre-teen years. I was due for a new coat. I knew exactly what I wanted. It was during WWII, and leather jackets, like the bomber pilots wore, were the 'in' thing. I wanted a flyer's jacket like my air force heroes wore. My mother, for some reason, was from another generation, and I was sure that generation was from another planet. She wanted me to have a long coat that came down to my knees. To her, this coat would be more practical than a flyer's jacket for several reasons. First, it was reversible and could also serve as a raincoat. Second, it was long and would keep my 'bottom' from freezing. Third, it was cheaper. Three strikes and I was out – Mom purchased the long coat.

Little did she know, but her troubles had just begun. Now, she had to get me to wear it. I detested the coat, so I avoided wearing it whenever I could. She thought it made her little boy look like a man, so she enforced her preference on me. I thought it made me look like a sissy, so I would wear an old ragged substitute whenever she wasn't looking. Why did I avoid this lovely, warm, and practical coat? Because it made me different! No one else in the whole school had one. In fact, I was sure no one in the whole world had a coat like it. It would surely make me peculiar in the worst sense of the word.

Israel didn't want to be different from other nations either. They determined to practice their plan as a substitute to God's plan. They would conform to the practices of other nations.

According to Webster's New World College Dictionary, to "conform" means to behave in a conventional way, accepting without question, customs, traditions, and prevailing opinions. In other words, it means we yield to the procedures of prevailing practices to avoid being peculiar. **God, however, is looking for a people who will dare to be different.** He's looking for people who will:

1) Commit to Him before they will commit to themselves

2) Focus on the eternal instead of the temporary

3) Learn to love as He loved, and give as He gave.

When God's people comply with His teachings, they will be peculiar in the best sense of the word. A person is different if he turns the other cheek when he is mistreated. He is unusual if he loves his enemies, or is special if he seeks God's Kingdom and the good of others before his own welfare. These are the kinds of people God is expecting His followers to be.

We, on the other hand, tend to pick and choose what we will and won't comply with. We have our own ideas of what a Christian should be, and when it conflicts with God's will, we substitute our own will for His.

Israel had their own idea of what a good nation should be. The Israelites were sure a good nation would consist of a mighty king to go out before them. Can you imagine how this made God feel? They ignored how He had mightily led them out of Egypt, across the Red Sea, through the wilderness, around Jericho, and into the Promised Land. Now, they wanted a substitute for God. They wanted a king. They crowned their king, but they rejected their God.

Are we any different from Israel in our quest for our spiritual achievement? We substitute self-righteousness for His imparted righteousness. We depend on good works in place of His grace. We emphasize emotional needs above spiritual needs, and we misconstrue socializing for evangelizing, ability for humility, contentment for commitment, and profession for possession.

We, like Israel, have found our own king, but we have lost our God. Our substitutes look right and sufficient, when they are all we have. We define, refine, and combine our ideas, but when all is said and done, we have said much and done little. That's because we have lost sight of doing things God's way and have substituted our way.

The only guideline we have, to show us what God expects from us, is His Word. The question is, "How willing are we to take these instructions seriously and endeavor to carry them out?" Are we willing to come out from among them and be a separate people? Are we zealous to be holy because He is holy? Are we agreeable to love our enemies and bless those who curse us? Are we seeking to be filled with the Holy Spirit? Are we preparing to "go into all the world" and make disciples of all nations?

In his book, "GROWING TRUE DISICPLES," George Barna makes some startling statements. He challenges us with these words, *"The Great Commission gets our juices flowing, doesn't it? It's marching orders from God. But how many Christians do you know whose articulated life purpose is to help fulfill that tremendous challenge? How many believers do you know who get out of bed every morning asking what they can do to show and tell people about Jesus, to make those people disciples of the Lord, and to act like true disciples themselves?"*

In one recent nationwide survey, we asked people to describe themselves as "Christian." Four out of ten said they were personally committed to Jesus Christ, had confessed their sins, and believe they will go to heaven after they die because of God's grace provided through Jesus' death and resurrection. But not one of the adults we interviewed said that their goal in life was to be a committed follower of Jesus Christ or to make disciples." (4)

This survey reveals a conspicuous failure on the part of Christians when you realize Jesus has commanded us to:

> "Go therefore and make disciples of all the nations, baptizing them
> in the name of the Father and of the Son and of the Holy Spirit."
> Matthew 28:19

The underlying cause of America's lackadaisical response to the Great Commission is that we have not made it a goal to be committed followers of Jesus Christ. We intend to serve the Lord on our own terms. When we dictate the terms of our commitment, we are guilty of substituting 'our way' for 'God's way.' We try hard to fit things together and make them work our way. We try to make it easy and convenient for the world to embrace our gospel, but we fail to make them true disciples of Jesus Christ.

Because we Christians fail as true Disciples of Christ, it is no wonder we miss the mark in the converts we produce. Sadly, Christians don't share some of God's standards with new converts in order to make it easy for them to accept our Gospel. We are already guilty of this blunder in our own lives, so it is easy to take it down another notch to a man-made standard, which of course is a substitute for God's standard. The problem is, our standards are getting lower and lower and our relationship to God is getting weaker and weaker. We find it easier and easier to fit in to the world around us. Fitting into the world is a part of our scheme. We adjust, reduce, substitute, and eliminate, until we have a standard that suits us. **After we begin to fit into the world, we try to fit God into this world with us.** God doesn't fit into this world, and neither will we if we are true disciples of Jesus Christ.

> *"Because God is so big and so great, even His followers*
> *are considered aliens and strangers in this world."*
> Hebrews 11:13 (NIV)

Jeremiah 2:13 (NIV) illustrates the futility of our substitutes compared to God's ways:

> *"My people have committed two sins. They have forsaken*
> *me, the spring of living water, and have dug their own*
> *cisterns, broken cisterns that cannot hold water."*

We are busy digging our own cisterns, but they will hold no water with God. We have our cisterns neatly packaged and readily available for our use. We have substituted promotion for prayer, socializing for evangelism, fellowship for discipleship, contentment for commitment, charisma for anointing, information for transformation, numerical growth for spiritual growth, head knowledge for heart experience, comfort for passion, tolerance for holiness, laurels for morals, emotions for worship, good intention for missions, psychology for theology, good works for grace, and tradition for truth.

Many churches are not interested in the truth unless it is their brand of truth. Anything that detracts from their already perceived persuasion is either heretical or unnecessary. **It is time for us to get back on track and start doing things God's way.** We must build a fresh relationship with God and stop trying to be so relevant to the world around us. To do this, we must bury our substitutes and resurrect the truth of God.

WAKE-UP CALL
Chapter 6

"But make sure that you don't get so absorbed and exhausted in taking care of all your day-by-day obligations that you lose track of the time and doze off, oblivious to God. The night is about over, the dawn is about to break. Be up and awake to what God is doing! God is putting the finishing touches on the salvation work he began when we first believed. We can't afford to waste a minute, must not squander these precious daylight hours in frivolity and indulgence, in sleeping around and dissipation, in bickering and grabbing everything in sight. Get out of bed and get dressed! Don't loiter and linger, waiting until the very last minute. Dress yourselves in Christ, and be up and about!"
ROMANS 13:11-14 (MSG) *His Buisness*

I read a true story about Larry Carter, president of Great Lakes Christian College, who, when he was a young fellow, played on a little league baseball team. Carter said that at the beginning of each season the coach would host a picnic for all the team members, and after they ate hot dogs and burgers, the coach would have them all sit down and he would give a pep talk. His first question to the boys was, **"How many of you have a dream of one day playing in the Major Leagues?"** Carter said that almost every boy's hand shot up. Every kid there believed that they could, one day, play in the Major Leagues. He said you could even see it in their eyes. The coach then told them, **"If that is to happen that dream must begin now!"** That inspired the boys so much that they practiced and played hard, and went undefeated for the next few seasons.

Twenty-five years later, Larry Carter became a Little League coach. He brought all his team together and gave them a pep talk – the same one his coach gave him. When he asked the same question, **"How many of** *you have a dream of one day playing in the Major Leagues,"* not one hand was raised. What was the difference? Not one kid believed he could do it. Carter said that you could see the defeat in their eyes. No one believed that anything great was ahead for him. Carter then asked himself, "What happened in the 25 years since he was a kid. What had come into the lives of those kids that stole their dreams and convinced them that they would never be more than what they were then?" (7)

That story reminded me of how Jesus took a band of His followers aside and said, *"How many of you will be a disciple of mine and spread my good news to a lost and dying world?"* Almost all their hands shot up. Every follower with his hand up believed he could do it. You could see it in their eyes. Jesus then told them:

> *"Go to Jerusalem and wait until you receive the power*
> *I will send you to accomplish your mission."*
> Luke 24:49

Those disciples obeyed His instruction and received the power He had promised and spread the good news of salvation to a lost and dying world. The all-star team from the world of darkness contended with them and lost. They accomplished such unbelievable miracles that they were accused of turning the world upside down. (Acts 17:6)

Two thousand years later a pastor stood in his pulpit and said, **"We need to reach out into this city and win the many lost and dying souls who need our message of salvation. How many of you will join our evangelism class and help to accomplish this mission?"** Not one hand was raised. Not one person believed he could do it. You could see it in their eyes; it was reflected in their lack of accomplishment. The pastor stood speechless.

What has happened to the Church of Jesus Christ? Where has our enthusiasm gone that once inspired us to take the challenge of Christ seriously and respond to it promptly? It would seem we are in a stupor and aimlessly wandering around in a state of unconsciousness. To put it bluntly, **the church has fallen asleep.**

The story is told about a pastor who was rather disappointed that things in the church were not happening like he wanted. He asked one of his leading deacons, **"What is wrong with our church? Is it ignorance or** *apathy?"* The deacon responded, *"I don't know and I don't care."* (1) The pastor was given more than an answer to his question; he was given a demonstration to it.

Apathy is an indication that the church is on its way to slumber-land. It may not be totally asleep but it is losing consciousness to a lost world; it is becoming indifferent to a fervent love for God; it is losing influence to a liberal environment that grows stronger as the church nods.

Probably the biggest obstacle the church has to overcome is apathy. Persecution is difficult to deal with but it seems to drive the Christian closer to God. Doctrinal differences have caused many churches to split but at least people do search the Word even if it is only to prove their point. Poverty keeps the church from attempting new ventures but it also keeps them on their knees. But when apathy sets in the church becomes drunk on the un-cola: unconscious, unmovable, and unconcerned.

Paul was obviously conscious of the apathy already prevalent in his day when he declared:

"And do this, knowing the time, that now it is high time to awake out of sleep; for now our salvation is nearer than when we first believed."
Romans 13:11

Paul was trying to stimulate the slumbering saints in his day and bring them back to a valid ministry under the leadership of the Holy Spirit. His exhortation in Romans is still valid for us today.

Jesus speaks to His disciples and tells them:

"Watch therefore, for you do not know what hour your Lord is coming. But know this, that if the master of the house had known what hour the thief would come, he would have watched and not allowed his house to be broken into. Therefore you also be ready, for the Son of Man is coming at an hour you do not expect."
Matthew 24:42-44

Strong's Exhaustive Concordance explains that the Greek word for "watch" in the text above is "gregoreuo," which means to keep awake, to be vigilant, to be alert. It is an instruction to be alert so that the coming of the

Lord doesn't take us unaware. The Greek word for "ready" is "hetoimos," which means to be prepared, made ready, to be fit, to be adjusted. It is an instruction to take care of all the details pertaining to the coming of the Lord.

These admonitions remind me of a race car driver who is getting things ready for a big race. He does everything he can to make himself awake and alert. Then he prepares the car to perform at its best. There are the last-minute adjustments and fine tuning so that the car will accomplish what it was built to do. This is a picture of what Jesus was saying to His disciples when He told them to "watch" and be "ready."

When we are asleep, in the physical sense, the eyes are usually closed and there is little or no conscious thought or voluntary movement, but there is intermitted dreaming. In other words, we are in a state of inactivity, and living in another world.

I have thought how similar this is to being asleep spiritually. We are not really conscious of spiritual things or to the Holy Spirit's prompting. We don't venture to make any spiritual strides or pursue any spiritual goals. We end up in another world of fantasy, dreaming of things that gratify our selfish ambitions. In this unholy state of unconsciousness many Christians are stumbling along hoping they are ready for the coming of the Lord.

Are we not sleeping when we have unsaved neighbors who are going to hell and we make no effort to tell them about a suffering Savior who died to take away their sins? Are we not sleeping when we can absent ourselves from the House of God for months at a time and not feel we are ignoring the admonition of Paul to not forsake the assembling of ourselves together? (Hebrews 10:25) Are we not sleeping when conditions around us indicate that the "perilous times" Paul predicted in II Timothy 3:1 would come in the last days, and yet we go on as though everything is as it should be? How about the internal disputing we hear about in churches? Disputes about music, procedures, policies, ethics, race, and buildings. I heard about one church that split over what color to paint the new bathroom. **It is no wonder that an observing world ignores our preaching because we do not exemplify it with our conduct.**

Before Jesus comes back for His church, He has a massive work of arousing, restoring, and commissioning to do in the slumbering 21st Century Christians who are oblivious to their condition and the need of the world around them.

The wonderful thing is that **God hasn't given up on His church**. God meant it when He said, *"I will build My church and the gates of Hades will not prevail against it."* Matthew 16:18. God is in the process of building and rebuilding His church to make it ready for His coming.

We see how the Spirit inspired Paul to write to Timothy and tell him, *"Therefore I remind you to stir up the gift of God, which is in you through the laying on of my hands. For God has not given us a spirit of fear, but of power and of love and of a sound mind."* II Timothy 1:6-7 Timothy was guilty of neglecting his gift because of a spirit of fear. He had backed off and had become inactive in the use of that gift, and this was a concern to the Lord. He had better things in mind for Timothy, so He inspired Paul to wake him up that he might utilize his gift to its full potential.

The church of Jesus Christ has not reached its full potential. There is a need for us to be stirred up and to get back to doing God's work, God's way.

When Peter failed his Lord and denied Him three times, God didn't give up on him. Peter wouldn't have qualified as a pastoral candidate at that time, but God wasn't finished with him yet. In expectation of Peter's restoration and future ministry, Jesus had to commission him again and prepare him for works still to be done. Jesus still had plans for Peter to become a useful instrument when He said:

"When you have returned to Me, strengthen your brethren."
Luke 22:32

God wasn't finished with Peter, but before Peter could have an effective ministry Jesus had to restore him from his fall and return him to his call. Jesus had to let him fall on his face so he would humbly return and faithfully carry out his renewed commission.

Oh, what a similarity we see between Peter and the church! We have made our bold claims that we couldn't keep. We have resorted to fleshly methods, only to see them bring added annoyance. We resigned our Great Commission and returned to our meager task of trying to keep the Old Gospel Ship from sinking. Like Peter, **we need to go out and "weep bitterly" and return to the Lord so that we might restore our walk with God and renew our commission to serve Him.**

Jonah is another servant of God who had to be restored to his commission from God. When God commissioned him to go to Nineveh the first time, he arose to flee to Tarshish. (Jonah 1:1-3) God had to send a storm and a fish to awaken this rebellious prophet and motivate him on his way to fulfilling his commission. His repentant prayer is recorded for us in Jonah 2:1-9.

The fish that swallowed Jonah discovered, "You can't keep a good man down," and at God's command, it vomited Jonah out onto dry ground. (Jonah 2:10) The story doesn't end there, God wasn't finished with Jonah; he needed an attitude adjustment. He thought God was too merciful to an undeserving and sinful people. Seeking to justify his act of rebellion in running away from his first call, Jonah reminded God:

"Was not this what I said when I was still in my country?
Therefore I fled previously to Tarshish; for I know that You are
a gracious and merciful God, slow to anger and abundant in
loving kindness, One who relents from doing harm."

Jonah 4:2

God went to great lengths to show this obstinate prophet that there is more to prophesying than to gain a favorable reputation. Jonah wanted to boast of having a 1000 batting average. When his batting average slumped he perched himself overlooking the city:

"Till he might see what would become of the city."

Jonah 4:5

The hot sun shown down upon Jonah's head, so God prepared a plant to shade him from his misery. I can imagine Jonah thanking the Lord over and over again for showing him mercy by giving him the comfort of shade for his head, but he, in turn, felt no mercy for the 120,000 people in Nineveh that he felt were not worth saving.

There was another step in God's plan to bring Jonah into line. He prepared a worm to gnaw away on the plant that shaded him until it withered and died. Then God prepared a hot east wind that focused again on Jonah's unprotected head, driving him to wish he were dead for the second time. The first time he wished he were dead because Nineveh wasn't destroyed. The second time he wished he were dead because the plant was destroyed, and he was no longer shaded. God had to show Jonah how inconsistent his mercy level was. He had more mercy for a dying plant than he did for 120,000 dying people.

The scripture account abruptly ends right there. I have some probing questions for you to consider. Was God finished with Jonah at that point? Was there any reason why God took such pains to correct Jonah's attitude? Did Jonah get a third chance to get it right?

Although answers to these questions would be sheer speculation I tend to think God wasn't finished with Jonah at that time. I believe God had a purpose for every lesson He taught Him, just as He does for us today. Certainly Jonah learned something about obeying God from his experience in the belly of the fish. Would it not be reasonable to believe God had further plans to use Jonah? God doesn't take such elaborate steps to train someone and then leave him to sit by the wayside. There must have been a further job for Jonah.

God has not given up on the church, in spite of its slumbering, stumbling, shaky existence.

> *"Christ also loved the church and gave Himself for her,*
> *that He might sanctify and cleanse her with the washing of*
> *water by the word, that He might present her to Himself*
> *a glorious church, not having spot or wrinkle or any such*
> *thing, but that she should be holy and without blemish."*
>
> Ephesians 5:25-27

God has not stopped loving the church and He's cleansing her to prepare her for the day of His coming. This work of purging and perfecting His church will intensify as we get closer to His coming. (I will address this matter in another chapter.)

What will it take for us to wake up? Some people sleep more deeply than others, and it takes a firmer shaking to awaken them. Others are light sleepers, and a slight jar will stir them out of slumber.

Perhaps you are one who is easily awakened, and you will stir yourself to action from just reading this book. On the other hand, you may be one who is sleeping deeply and needs to pray, *'God shake me up and wake me up so I'll be ready for you to take me up.'*

Danny Cox, a former jet-pilot turned business leader, teaches that when jet fighters were manufactured they had greater speed then planes with propellers. In jet fighters, pilot ejection needed to be more sophisticated, although in theory, all a pilot really needed to do was push a button and get out of the seat so his parachute would open. But, there was a problem that popped up during testing of the ejection system. Some pilots, instead of letting go, would keep a grip on the seat. The parachute would remain trapped between the seat and the pilot's back.

So, the engineers went back to the drawing board and came up with a solution. The new design called for a two-inch webbed strap. One end attached to the front edge of the seat under the pilot. The other end attached to an electronic take-up reel behind the headrest. Two seconds after ejection, the electronic take-up reel would immediately take up the slack and force the pilot forward out of his seat thus freeing the parachute.

Bottom line? Jet fighter pilots needed that device to launch them out of their chairs in an emergency. (1)

What will it take to launch us out of our sleep?

JUDGMENT BEGINS AT HOME!

Chapter 7

> *"For it is time for judgment to begin with the family of God; and if it begins with us, what will the outcome be for those who do not obey the gospel of God?"*
>
> I PETER 4:17 (NIV)

Allen Adams had a bad day on September 8, 1996. On that particular Sunday, he was watching the Pittsburgh Steelers play the Baltimore Ravens in Three Rivers Stadium. At halftime, Adams was one of the fans chosen to come onto the field and attempt a field goal. The promotional contest let these lucky fans try to win either a free dinner at a very exclusive restaurant or round-trip airline tickets. During the contest, another fan took an interest in Adams's trip to the playing field. When Sergeant John Kearney heard Adams's name announced over the loudspeakers, he called his office to confirm a warrant for the arrest of this "would-be field goal kicker." As Adams walked off the field, Sergeant Kearney arrested him for a previous assault charge. (5)

It would seem that Allen Adams thought he had escaped the responsibility of being accountable for his conduct. Justice delayed is not justice removed. Sooner or later your sin will find you out.

We all have stood in wonderment as we watched people commit one transgression after another and seem to get away with it without being held accountable for their actions. We have seen others who transgressed once and were cut down on the spot. Understandably we ask the question, why does God vary His demonstration of justice so unevenly?

Scripture teaches us that **God doesn't always immediately administer judgment for doing wrong:**

"The sins of some men are obvious, reaching the place of judgment ahead of them; the sins of others trail behind them."
II Timothy 5:24 (NIV)

God's system of justice may not be like ours and often we don't understand it. But we must remember God says,

"As the heavens are higher than the earth, so are My ways higher than your ways, and My thoughts than your thoughts."
Isaiah 55:9

We must come to know that God is fair and just in all that He does. We read in Psalm 98:9 (NIV), **"He will judge the world in righteousness and the peoples with equity."** We may not understand how, why, or when God's justice is administered, but we must be assured it is done in the right way at the right time.

There is a Day of Judgment coming for the ungodly at the Great White Throne Judgment. *"Then I saw a great white throne and Him who sat on it, from whose face the earth and the heaven fled away. And there was found no place for them. And I saw the dead, small and great, standing before God, and books were opened. And another book was opened, which is the Book of Life. And the dead were judged according to their works, by the things which were written in the books. The sea gave up the dead who were in it, and Death and Hades delivered up the dead who were in them. And they were judged, each one according to his works. Then Death and Hades were cast into the lake of fire. This is the second death. And everyone not found written in the Book of Life was cast into the lake of fire."* Revelation 20:11-15 The Book of Life is opened to show the ungodly that their names are not found among the names of the godly that are written within the Book.

The lives of Christians are to be judged at the Judgment Seat of Christ. *"For we must all appear before the judgment seat of Christ, that each one may receive the things done in the body, according to what he has done, whether good or bad."* II Corinthians 5:10 This judgment is not to determine whether the person goes to heaven or not but to determine whether their works are deserving of reward.

Often God gives a demonstration of judgment as an example so we will know what is coming in the final analysis. We read about it in Luke 13:1-5: *"There were present at that season some who told Him about the Galileans whose blood Pilate had mingled with their sacrifices. And Jesus answered and said to them, 'Do you suppose that these Galileans were worse sinners than all other Galileans, because they suffered such things? I tell you, no; but unless you repent you will all likewise perish.' Or those eighteen, on whom the tower in Siloam fell and killed them, do you think that they were worse sinners than all other men who dwelt in Jerusalem? I tell you, no; but unless you repent you will all likewise perish.'"*

The point to recognize here is that **Jesus used these catastrophic calamities as an example of coming judgment for those who didn't repent of their sins.** It was not that these who experienced these calamities were any worse in their conduct than others around them, but all who saw this witnessed an example of what God's ultimate judgment would be like for those who didn't repent.

The account of Ananias and Sapphira in Acts 5:1-11 is another illustration of God's judgment. This couple sold a piece of property and kept back part of the proceeds for themselves. Not that this was wrong, but they both made it appear as if they had given the whole amount to the Lord, and thus they lied to God. For this deceptive act against God they both fell dead in the presence of Peter.

The sudden deaths of Ananias and Sapphira affected the observers with fear and respect. *"...everyone who heard of these things had a healthy respect for God. They knew God was not to be trifled with."* Acts 5:11 (Msg) *"But even though people admired them* (believers) *a lot, outsiders were wary about joining them."* Acts 5:13 (Msg) This was one church you didn't join on a whim. Qualifications were demanding and the stakes were high.

God had His reasons for making an example of Ananias and Sapphira at the very beginning of the church. He wanted all of us to know we are dealing with a just and exacting God. What happened to Ananias and Sapphira is what will happen to all of us if we disregard the mercy of God. God doesn't immediately mete out judgment for evils done today. If He did we wouldn't have to wait for financial, sexual and abusive behavior to be exposed. The offender would fall dead on the scene, and the next person would think twice before he indulged his flesh.

I believe that God will again demonstrate His style of judgment in the last days of the church age. In many ways, God has already begun this through the exposure of those who are deceiving the public through their practices of fraud, displays of jealousy, and their acts of adultery.

God is longsuffering, patient, and merciful toward us in dealing with our sins. It is stated very succinctly in II Peter 3:6 (Msg), *"He is restraining himself on account of you, holding back the End because he doesn't want anyone lost. He is giving everyone space and time to change."* There will come an end to that restraining power, and when it comes we will have to reckon with the judgment of God.

Centuries ago, a man conned his way into the Chinese emperor's orchestra. He could not play the flute, but he dramatically mimicked the characteristics of a seasoned flutist. His charade afforded him a modest salary and a comfortable place to live. He enjoyed the trappings of his deception until the emperor decided he would like to hear a private solo from each musician in the orchestra. In a state of panic, he took flute lessons, but he couldn't learn fast enough. In desperation, he feigned illness, but the court physician couldn't find anything wrong with him. On the eve before his presentation, this con artist took poison and committed suicide. The Chinese language was impacted by this historical event, and it has impacted the English language as well. Because of that situation we now have the phrase, *"He refused to face the music."* (5)

The day is coming when we all will have to "face the music." If we don't face it in this life we will face it in the life to come. We have to be made accountable for our actions; therefore, we should refrain from transgressing the commandments of God.

Rachael Kovac was taught an unusual way to "face the music." After being ticketed twice for speeding, the seventeen-year-old resident of St. Joseph, Missouri, received a special bumper sticker from her parents in March of 1999. Concerned over their daughter's driving record, Dennis and Cindy Kovac attached a powerful message to Rachael's car, which read, *"If I'm Speeding, Call My Parents!"* It then listed the family phone number. This accountability sticker garnered the results Mr. and Mrs. Kovac desired because Rachel quit speeding. (5)

I think we all would be willing to change our life style if our conduct was publicized that blatantly. But God gives us room to repent and time to change and does not take pleasure in putting us in our place.

We know from Ephesians 5:25 that *"Christ loved the church and gave Himself for it."* We further know **"Whom the Lord loves He chastens."** Hebrews. 12:6 With this in mind I contend that God has obligated Himself to deal with the carnal pursuits of a wayward church.

Peter explores this truth in I Peter 4:17, *"For the time has come for judgment to begin at the house of God; and if it begins with us first, what will be the end of those who do not obey the gospel of God?"* Peter is making a case that God, who loves the church, will bring judgment upon it to purge and prepare it to perform effective ministry to a lost and dying world. The word "time" means a set or proper time, an opportunity, a due season. Peter is saying, *"The house of God is due for judgment to sanctify and cleanse the bride for the coming groom."*

If judgment must begin at the house of God first, that means it must begin here and now! We must line up with the Word of God, follow the leadership of the Holy Spirit, and harmonize our efforts with the rest of God's people. When we do this, we will emerge a renewed and revitalized people, zealous to accomplish God's work. A restored church will then have an impact on an ungodly world. Some will repent and be spared the judgment of eternal separation from God.

God's main concern on planet earth today is His Church. He is building His Church and increasing its numbers. He is courting His bride and getting her ready for the great wedding day. We read in Ephesians 5:25-27, *"Christ loved the church and gave Himself for her, that He might sanctify and cleanse her with the washing of water by the word, that He might present her to Himself a glorious church, not having spot or wrinkle or any such thing, but that she should be holy and without blemish."* This process of sanctifying and cleansing is going on presently. I believe this process will intensify as we approach the coming of the Lord.

Strong's Exhaustive Concordance explains that the Greek word for church is "ekklesia," which means the "called out" ones. When a person responds to Christ's salvation and separates himself from the world, this "calling out" qualifies him to become a part of the church and receive God's special care and attention. The Greek word "sanctify" means to consecrate, to set apart as holy. When God sets the born again believer apart He designates him for special care and attention. John 15:2 proclaims, *"Every branch in Me that does not bear fruit He takes away; and every branch that bears fruit He prunes, that it may bear more fruit."* As a gardener prunes away the dead and unproductive branches of a fruit tree, to make it more productive, so the Lord prunes away the useless and unproductive products of our lives so that we may become more fruitful in spiritual results.

The church is an example to the world of what a child of God is like or should be like. Paul reminds us:

> *"Your very lives are a letter that everyone can read by just looking at you. Christ himself wrote it – not with ink, but with God's living Spirit; not chiseled into stone, but carved into human lives – and we publish it."*
>
> II Corinthians 3:2-5 (Msg)

God wants the world to know what His children are like. I think of how God called attention to Job when He said to Satan, *"Have you considered my servant Job, that there is none like him on the earth, a blameless and upright man, one who fears God and shuns evil?"* Job 1:8 I think God was bragging a little on His son Job because he was exemplary in his behavior and a good example to all who wanted to see his blameless life, his upright conduct, and his holy fear of the God.

Are we, the church, giving a good example to the world? Does God employ His bragging rights about us? I am afraid what happens in the church is anything but what He would want to brag about; immorality, fraud, deceit, division, lack of forgiveness, and the list could go on. Sometimes I think it is Satan who says to God, *"Have you considered your servant _____? He is up to his old tricks again."* We do know Satan is the, *"Accuser of our brethren, who accused them before our God day and night."* Revelation 12:10

The world, also, is quick to expose the failure of one of God's children and shoot them down in the public eye. The disgrace weakens the church's influence and grieves the heart of the Lord, while the devil looks on and gloats. However, as God purifies His church, somewhere along the way there will be a good example displayed for their investigation. Those who want to be persuaded will have their opportunity to believe and those who refuse to be persuaded will continue to magnify the failures of God's people.

God is acutely aware of the example we project to the on looking world. I am sure it grieves Him more than it does us when one of His children leaves a scandalous example for the world to criticize. God will do something to protect the family name, hence, *"The time has come for judgment to begin at the house of God."* I Peter 4:17 God is going to "clean up" His Church before He comes to "take up" His Church.

The church is here to be an example to an observing world. The story is told of a T. V. repairman who didn't like to think about his job when he came home. As a result, he never bothered to properly install the T. V. antenna on the top of his house or fix it when one arm broke in a windstorm. One day a new family moved in next door, and the owner went up on his roof to install a new antenna. Knowing that his neighbor was a T. V. repairman, he put his up exactly the same way and turned his antenna to face in the same direction as his neighbor's. Then, after studying his neighbor's antenna for a while, he reached up and broke one arm off his antenna! (3) What kind of example was his neighbor?

As Children of God, we teach by example, whether we intend to or not. We don't always know the impression the world is getting from the lives we live. What kind of world would this be if people followed your demonstration of Christian living in every aspect? Can you recommend your style of Christian living to the unsaved people around you?

Jesus said, *"Let me tell you why you are here. You're here to be salt-seasoning that brings out the God-flavor of this earth. If you lose you saltiness, how will people taste godliness? You've lost your usefulness and will end up in the garbage. Here's another way to put it: You're here to be light, bringing out the God-colors in the world. God is not a secret to be kept. We're going public with this, as public as a city on a hill. If I make you light-bearers, you don't think I'm going to hide you under a bushel, do you? I'm putting you on a light stand – shine! Keep open house, be generous with your lives. By opening up to others, you'll prompt people to open up with God, this generous Father in heaven."*

Matthew 5:13-16 (Msg)

We are here to give flavor to the taste of godliness in this world. People are wanting to: ***"taste and see that the Lord is good."*** Psalm 34:8 The flavor we exhibit will either attract people to God, or it will drive people away from God. Often people get a bad taste of what a Christian is and are turned away from ever becoming a Christian. God is displeased with this and seeks to bring us back to a tasteful example to the world.

As salt we are also a preserving agent. Lot was a deterrent to God's judgment on Sodom and Gomorrah. The Angels of the Lord had to hasten Lot and his wife and daughters out of Sodom. As long as they remained there the judgment couldn't fall. Likewise, the church has been a deterrent to the judgment of God falling on this earth and will be until Jesus comes. We are the influence that preserves this world and makes it a tolerable place to live.

Not only is the church salt to preserve and give a good flavor to the gospel, it is also light to put God on display and to give people guidance to find Him. We are "light bearers" who are to reveal the goodness and greatness of God to all who would seek Him. Without this light the world would be a dark and morbid place to exist.

Paul writes to Titus and tells him, ***"In all things showing yourself to be a pattern of good works; in doctrine showing integrity, reverence, incorruptibility."*** Titus 2:7 We are a pattern for people to follow. If we are not a good pattern illustrating the true character of Jesus Christ people will have a perverted concept of what a Christian is. God doesn't want people to have a twisted idea about holy living so He is duty bound to alter our pattern of Him so people will get the true picture. That's why, **"judgment must begin at the house of God"** so we will become the influence to the world that will bring people to God.

God has given us room to judge ourselves. Paul instructs us to, ***"Test yourselves to make sure you are solid in the faith. Don't drift along taking everything for granted. Give yourselves regular checkups. You need first hand evidence, not mere hearsay, that Jesus Christ is in you. Test it out. If you fail the test, do something about it."*** II Corinthians 13:5 (Msg)

We can do something about our spiritual condition if we take the initiative to do it. The problem is we drift along, taking for granted that because judgment hasn't fallen, everything is all right. Everything may not be all right.

Every year I have a physical checkup. I go to the doctor and he pokes and prods me and examines parts of me I have never even heard about. When all is finished, he gives me the anxiously awaited news. Sometimes he tells me, *"You passed, all is well."* That makes me feel very good and relieved. Sometimes he has instructions for me to follow, *"Change your diet, stay away from sugar, exercise more, stop worrying, and take these pills."* I may not be happy about what I have to do to stay healthy but I pay good money to this guy to make these recommendations to me, and he's only doing his job so I heed his advice.

I know of many people who avoid these yearly checkups. They take for granted that because they can function normally and live an active life they are all right physically. One day a pain begins to develop and finally they are forced to visit the doctor. After a thorough examination they get the diagnosis; they have cancer. And then they hear those regretful words, *"If only you would have come in earlier we could have treated this condition and prevented this terrible consequence."*

Are you having frequent spiritual checkups? How is your forgiveness level? How are you treating your enemies? Where is your love level? How effective is your witness to the lost? Are you caught up on your tithes? Is your prayer life producing powerfully? It is time for judgment to begin at the house of God. You take the initiative and ask God to, *"Search me, O God, and know my heart: try me, and know my thoughts: And see if there be some wicked way in me, and lead me in the way everlasting."* Psalm 139:23-24 (KJV)

SHAKEN LOOSE!
Chapter 8

"So don't turn a deaf ear to these gracious words. If those who ignored earthly warnings didn't get away with it, what will happen to us if we turn our backs on heavenly warnings? His voice that time shook the earth to its foundations; this time - he's told us this quite plainly - he'll also rock the heavens: 'One last shaking, from top to bottom, stem to stern.' The phrase, 'one last shaking' means a thorough house-cleaning, getting rid of all the historical and religious junk so that the unshakable essentials stand clear and uncluttered. Do you see what we've got? An unshakable kingdom! And do you see how thankful we must be? Not only thankful, but brimming with worship, deeply reverent before God. For God is not an indifferent bystander. He's actively cleaning house, torching all that needs to burn, and he won't quit until it's all cleansed. God himself is a fire!"

HEBREWS 12:25-29 (MSG)

Long ago, in the days of sailing ships, a terrible storm arose and a ship was lost at sea. Only one crewman survived; he washed up on a small uninhabited island. In his desperation, the castaway daily prayed to God for help and deliverance from his lonely existence. Each day he looked for a passing ship and saw nothing. Eventually he managed to build a crude hut, in which he stored the few things he had recovered from the wreck and those things he had made to help him. One day, as the sailor was returning from his daily search for food, he saw a column of smoke. As he ran toward it he saw that his hut was in flames. All was lost. Now, not only was he alone, but he had nothing to help him in his struggle for survival. Stunned and nearly overcome with grief and despair, he fell into a deep depression and spent a nearly sleepless night wondering what was to become of him and questioning whether life itself was even worth the effort.

The next morning, he rose early and went down to the sea. There, to his amazement, he saw a ship lying offshore and a small boat rowing toward him. When the once-marooned man met the ship's captain, he asked him how he had known to send help. The captain replied, *"Why, we saw your smoke signal yesterday, but by the time we drew close the tide was against us. So we had to wait until now to come and get you."* (3)

God has a way of working calamities together for our good. They may entail pain and loss for the present, but in the long run God brings them around to benefit us. Sometimes the route to the answers to our prayers necessitates burning up what we depend on so God can bring us to the source of help that never fails: Himself.

The ultimate message of Hebrews 12:25-29 is the future renovation of the atmospheric heavens and earth which is described for us in II Peter 3:10-13, *"But the day of the Lord will come as a thief in the night, in which the heavens will pass away with a great noise, and the elements will melt with fervent heat; both the earth and the works that are in it will be burned up. Therefore, since all these things will be dissolved, what manner of persons ought you to be in holy conduct and godliness, looking for and hastening the coming of the day of God, because of which the heavens will be dissolved, being on fire, and the elements will melt with fervent heat? Nevertheless we, according to His promise, look for new heavens and a new earth in which righteousness dwells."* This ultimate renovation that introduces the new heaven and the new earth chronologically comes after the Great White Throne Judgment and just prior to the presentation of the New Jerusalem. This would place it long after the rapture and just after the millennial reign of Christ. (Revelation 20:11 and 21:2)

The more immediate message of Hebrews 12:25-29 is a warning to hear the voice of God speaking to us in our time. If the voice of God shook the earth at Mt. Sinai, how much more will his voice shake the earth and heaven in light of His work at Calvary? We saw how the earth was shaken through a tsunami in 2004 and thousands were lost. What will happen when God shakes the earth?

Peter emphasized that the realization of the coming renovation is meant to be a motivating factor: *"Since all these things will be dissolved, what manner of persons ought you to be in holy conduct and godliness?"*

II Peter 3:11 The motivation of fear also enters into the picture: *"Since we are receiving a kingdom which cannot be shaken, let us have grace, by which we may serve God, acceptable with reverence and godly fear."* Hebrews 12:28

We have lost our fear of God. It seems people are quick to replace the word "fear" with "a feeling of awe", "to hold in reverence", "to have respect for", all of which are very true. Moreover, people seem to avoid the use of the expression, "fear", when it relates to God and rather portray Him as "a kind, benevolent, generous friend." The latter descriptions also are true but we must remember that God is also holy, just, and exacting. He is our Heavenly Father and will discipline us when we get out of line.

In our effort to make God more approachable, we have contrived a buddy to buddy relationship that we can feel at home with. We have demoted him to our level and have little reason to fear Him. As a result we think we can do pretty much as we please without fear of retribution. People are promiscuous, proud, and perverted in their conduct, and they blatantly parade this in the very face of a holy God. They are not afraid of God, and maybe the church has been guilty of squelching this truth.

Please don't think I am suggesting that we should cower and quake as we come before God. I am aware that Hebrews 4:16 tells us *"we can approach the throne of grace boldly or confidently and find mercy and grace in time of need."* This, however, does not negate the fact that we should maintain a healthy attitude of Godly fear – the fear that we would disappoint our Lord.

As a pastor, I counseled a couple who were guilty of adultery. The man was married and the woman was divorced. I reminded them that their acts of adultery were sin and that they should repent of this. The lady quickly assured me that she did repent, in fact, she said, *"I am repenting while I am doing it."* This lady had a perverted concept of the fear of God. She thought she could get away with sinning by just saying a quick "forgive me" prayer, but she forgot that God said that we must turn away from our sin if we are to be forgiven. (Isaiah 55:7)

Let me share a few of the many verses from the bible that instruct us about the fear of God.

"And now, Israel, what does the Lord your God require of you, but to fear the Lord your God, to walk in all His ways and to love Him, to serve the Lord your God with all your heart and with all your soul."
Deuteronomy 10:12

"The fear of the Lord is the beginning of wisdom…"
Psalm 111:10

"The fear of the Lord is the beginning of knowledge…"
Proverbs 1:7

"The fear of the Lord is to hate evil…"
Proverbs 8:13

"…by the fear of the Lord one departs from evil."
Proverbs 16:6

"It is a fearful thing to fall into the hands of a living God."
Hebrews 10:31

"And if you call on the Father, who without partiality judges according to each one's work, conduct yourselves throughout the time of your stay here in fear."
I Peter 1:17

"Honor all people. Love the brotherhood. Fear God. Honor the king."
I Peter 2:17

"…Fear God and give glory to Him, for the hour of His judgment has come…"
Revelation 14:7

Many of these verses inform us that fearing God is a motivating factor that keeps one from evil. If this fear were defined merely as awe or respect it wouldn't be much of a motivating force

God is speaking to us in these last days through shaking events that should motivate us to clean up our act and prepare for His coming. The shaking will intensify as time progresses because the need for it will become more and more necessary.

God spoke to us through the events of September 11, 2001. I am not saying that God planned and instigated these tragedies, but I am saying that God allowed it to happen. God didn't have to instigate this event – evil people contrived it. Incidents similar to those that occurred on 9/11 will intensify because:

"evil men and imposters will grow worse and worse."
II Timothy 3:13

It is important that we understand that **God speaks to people through catastrophic weather conditions.** God sent thunder, hail, and fire upon Egypt to motivate Pharaoh to release Israel from their bondage. (Exodus 9:23,28) Many scriptures describe a storm as being God's voice:

"The Lord thundered from heaven, And the Most High uttered His voice."
I Samuel 22:14

"Hear attentively the thunder of His voice, And the rumblings that comes from His mouth. God thunders marvelously with His voice; He does great things which we cannot comprehend."
Job 37:2, 5

"The Lord thundered from heaven, And the Most High uttered His voice, hailstones and coals of fire. Then the channels of the sea were seen, the fountains of the world were uncovered at your rebuke, O Lord, At the blast of the breath of Your nostrils."
Psalm 18:13-15
(Could verse 15 describe a Tsunami?)

"The voice of the Lord is over the waters; The God of glory thunders; The Lord is over many waters. The voice of the Lord is powerful; The voice of the Lord is full of majesty."
Psalm 29:3-4

My purpose for including all these scriptures is to assure you that God controls the storms and speaks through them to the hearts of men. *"The Lord has His way in the whirlwind and in the storm. And the clouds are the dust of His feet. He rebukes the sea and makes it dry, And dries up all the rivers. Bashan and Carmel wither. And the flower of Lebanon wilts."* Nahum 1:3-4 There should be no question in the faithful Christian's mind that God is able to literally do all of these things.

Much of the church in America today is soft, undisciplined, compromising, lazy, pathetic, and apathetic. It would seem to me that **the time has come for God to sanctify and cleanse His bride to prepare her for His coming.**

In his book, "The Empty Church," Thomas C. Reeves says, *"Christianity in America…tends to be easy, upbeat, convenient, and compatible. It does not require self-sacrifice, discipline, humility, an otherworldly outlook, a zeal for souls, a fear as well as love of God… What we now have might best be labeled 'Consumer Christianity.' The cost is low and customer satisfaction seems guaranteed."* (9) This is a sample of the "pick and choose" mentality many Christians practice in their commitment to Christ. The cross deals with our sins, not for our gratification.

Many Christians seem to pick and choose what they will and what they won't accept. If it doesn't suit or gratify their spiritual preferences, they are quick to reject it.

Because God loves us, He will ruffle our comfortable nest and shake up our complacent attitude to bring us to faithful commitment.

> *"Whom the Lord loves He chastens, and scourges every son whom He receives. If you endure chastening, God deals with you as with sons; for what son is there whom a father does not chasten? But if you are without chastening, of which all have become partakers, then you are illegitimate and not sons."*
>
> Hebrews 12:6-8

That reminds me of the following story. A father put his small boy to bed one evening.

[Five minutes later] ***"Da-ad…"***

"What?"

"I'm thirsty. Can you bring me a drink of water?"
"No. You had your chance. Lights out."
[Five minutes later] *"Da-aaaad."*
"What?"
"I'm thirsty. Can I have a drink of water?"
"I told you no! If you ask again, I'll have to spank you!"
[Five minutes later] *"Daaaa-aaaAAAAD..."*
"WHAT?"
"When you come in to spank me, can you bring me a drink of water?" (2)

Now that kid was really asking for a spanking and when he got it I don't think he said, *"Thanks dad, I really needed that."* Remember! When God fails to discipline us it is an indication that He doesn't even consider us to be His child.

I like the way Eugene Peterson's paraphrased bible, "The Message," interprets Hebrews 12:27, *"The phrase 'one last shaking' means a thorough housecleaning, getting rid of all the historical and religious junk so that the unshakable essentials stand clear and uncluttered."* The church certainly contains a lot of useless and deficient clutter that God is going to have to shake loose. We have substituted program for power, profession for possession, performance for persuasion, presentation for proclamation, and piety for purity. All this pointless paraphernalia will presently be plundered in God's providence.

When my wife, Virginia, and I retired, we moved to a smaller home in the quiet woods of northern Michigan. The size of the house made space a primary concern for us. Where to put everything became a dilemma. We piled boxes in closets, in the garage, in an empty bedroom and, still, there was more. We built two storage sheds and they were soon filled. Every winter we would promise each other that when the weather warmed up, we would work in the sheds and get rid of all that clutter. Many warm summers have come and gone and we are still looking at our scattered clutter. It's going to take a whole lot of shaking up to gain control over our chaos.

Some people hire professional cleaners who specialize in coming in and helping to remove household clutter. God calls forth and equips those He has specified to help clean up the clutter in His house. They are a voice in the wilderness crying, *"Prepare ye the way of the Lord."* Luke 3:4 (KJV) We need to give heed and hear God's message through them.

The church is in need of a thorough housecleaning to get rid of all the historical and religious junk. We have cluttered God's eternal blueprint with our temporary sketch and perverted the outcome of His providential work of grace.

When you touch a person's pocketbook, you touch a vital nerve that seems to be connected to their computerized security alarm button. They will do just about anything to protect their financial interests. The news recently reported about a woman who was shot to death by a thief because she refused to let go of her pocketbook. The thief was quickly apprehended with the pocketbook that contained less than $100. She put a higher value on her meager money than she did her priceless life.

God knows that *"Where your treasure is, there your heart will be also."* Luke 12:34 For many people, their treasure is not people, nor is it God, it is their earthly possessions. God knows where our heart is and often He will knock the financial props out from under us to help us get our attention back on Him.

Jesus said, *"It is more blessed to give than it is to receive."* Acts 20:35 Throughout His teachings, Jesus puts the primary focus on the joy of giving whereas we are more interested in the return we get, the "what's in it for me" philosophy.

American Christians are particularly vulnerable to the prosperity teaching of today. There is enough truth in this teaching to make it very appealing to our economic mindset, and highly deceptive to our blind quest for financial advantage. We all have probably heard the old adage, "You can't take it with you so send it on ahead." Some people have changed this by just adding one letter to send: "You can't take it with you so spend it on ahead."

Paul gives us some challenging instructions:

"Tell those rich in this world's wealth to quit being so full of themselves and so obsessed with money, which is here today and gone tomorrow. Tell them to go after God, who piles on all the riches we could ever manage – to do good, to be rich in helping others, to be extravagantly generous. If they do that, they'll build a treasury that will last, gaining life that is truly life."

I Timothy 6:17-19 (Msg)

This is an instruction to those who have wealth to invest it in the lives of others, and they will have a secure eternal return.

God gives us the power to get wealth (Deuteronomy 8:18). If this is true, God also can take that power away and give us poverty. I think God would prefer to give us wealth, but if our wealth causes us to lose sight of God, He can shake up our economic world and bring us back to dependence on Him.

Hebrews 12:1 tells us we should lay aside every weight, and the sin which so easily ensnares us, and to run with endurance the race that is set before us. In this instruction we are the ones who should take the initiative. The problem is that we don't have enough resolve to take the initiative. Even when we know we have to change and even make an attempt to do it, we don't carry through to the end. I think the reason for this is that we are duped by a soft, come easy, materialistic mentality that surrounds our everyday lives. We can have just about anything we want, if we work hard enough, or yell loud enough.

It's not likely the church is going to cleanse itself and get rid of its clutter. **God is going to have to help us get rid of our "junk"** by shaking us loose from our comfortable and convenient conditions. Even though we want to change and try to change, we just don't have the fortitude to break loose from our complacent inclination.

When God withdraws His restraining hand there will be catastrophes of all kinds that will unfold upon the earth. The book of Revelation gives a vivid picture of events that will happen on earth under God's orchestration. We are given a picture of wars and death, pestilence and plagues, cosmic convulsions and cataclysmic destruction, trumpets of trouble, and bowls of wrath. Christians who hold to the pre-tribulation rapture teaching interpret most of these events to happen after the rapture of the church. However, I am not sure that our escapism mentally can assure us we will avoid all the trouble that I believe has already started.

While Jesus was teaching about the destruction of the temple, His disciples asked Him to tell them when these things would happen and what the sign of His coming would be at the end of the age. (Matthew 24:1-3) Jesus said that many individuals would come claiming that they were the Christ (v.5). He told about wars and rumors of wars, about nation rising up against nation (v.6, 7). He spoke about famines, pestilence, and earthquakes. We must realize that these things are already happening. Jesus then adds, **"All these things are the beginning of sorrows."** Matthew 24:8 This beginning of sorrows literally means "birth-pains" and describes the travail that precedes actual birth. It would be difficult for me to believe that the church would escape all of these adverse events. I believe that the church will face a shaking time of hardship and adversity before the rapture takes place. To me this is necessary to shake us loose from our careless living and reckless attitude.

In Eugene Peterson's rendition of Hebrews 12:28-29 (Msg) we are informed that:

"He's actively cleaning house, torching all that needs to burn, and he won't quit until it's all cleansed. God himself is Fire!"

This is an ongoing process God is accomplishing in the church to prepare her for her eternal estate in heaven. The need for this cleansing is increasingly apparent as we observe the painful shortcomings the church portrays in its lackadaisical laziness, and apathetic attitude.

We are reminded:

"Christ also loved the church and gave Himself for her,
that He might sanctify and cleanse her with the washing of
water by the word, that He might present her to Himself
a glorious church, not having spot or wrinkle or any such
thing, but that she might be holy and without blemish."

Ephesians 5:25-27

It is obvious to me that the church is not yet pure and holy, being able to exemplify the glorious church God wants her to be.

The church is miserably failing in her mission to demonstrate the way of Christ to the world and to win the lost to salvation. Rob Hoskins, the Executive Director of the ministry of the Book of Hope, preached February 5, 2005 at the 21st Century Evangelism Explosion Conference, and stated that the statistics used to show that about 20% of all Christians did 80% of the giving, praying, and going – today that has fallen to 12% of all Christians doing any effective work for the Lord.

The only way the church will get back on course and fulfill her reason for being is to have God shake her up to get rid of all the 'religious junk' that she's hauling around so that the unshakable essentials can emerge clear and uncluttered.

God has to shake these things loose from our involuntary grasp because we don't possess the fortitude to break loose from these domineering influences. Too long we have allowed ourselves to fall into a mechanical way of worship not allowing the Spirit of God to move in our services. We have either become too formal with formatted services or we have gone to emotional extremes trying to satisfy everyone.

If we are to be ready for the coming of the Lord, we must respond correctly to His shaking process:

"At the time, discipline isn't much fun. It always feels like it's going against the grain. Later, of course, it pays off handsomely, for it's the well-trained who find themselves mature in their relationship with God."

Hebrews 12:11 (Msg)

When God deals with us in disciplinary actions, we recoil and retreat in displeasure from the experience hoping we can escape the unpleasant circumstances. God, however, is dealing with us for our own benefit and will not cancel the procedure until the lesson is learned. All of this is done to get us ready for better things.

We are in God's training program. He is getting us ready for the final battle. When we have endured the discipline of His shaking, we will be a "well-trained" army, ready for final action. Are you ready for training?

Blessed Affliction
Chapter 9

"Before I was afflicted I went astray, But now I keep your word."
PSALM 119:67

"It is good for me that I have been afflicted, that I may learn Your statutes."
PSALM 119:71

"I know, O Lord, that your judgments are right, And that in faithfulness You have afflicted me."
PSALM 119:75

During the summer of 1988, Yellowstone National Park suffered the worst fire of its history. A severe drought set the dramatic stage for lightning strikes in May. In late June, new fires erupted on the east and west sides of the park. By late July, the roaring fires were a daily feature on the news. On July 27, Interior Secretary Donald Hodel ordered a full-scale assault on the fires. Twenty-five thousand firefighters were deployed, 117 aircraft were put into the air and more than $120 million dollars in government spending was invested in battling these unbelievable fires.

However, 10 years later experts were humming a different tune. In 1998, officials said, **"By nearly every measure, the park is stronger now than before."** The park is filled with new life and growth even though officials didn't plant any new trees. The fires that effectively removed much of the dead wood and undergrowth also left an enriched soil that has accelerated new growth. (5)

The fires of affliction tend to shake loose those things that can be shaken so the things that cannot be shaken may remain. The things that remain will be healthier, stronger and more durable than anything we have known before. When the fires have passed, we learn as the Psalmist did that **affliction will teach us His ways and leave us with a blessing.**

The question "Does God afflict His people?" has to be settled before we can pursue this subject any further. If God is only interested in prosperity, health, and blessing for His people, then we must lay to rest the idea that He would afflict His people to bring them to holiness and cleansing.

If, on the other hand, God is interested in the church being a victorious, overcoming church, cleansed from worldliness and accomplishing His work on earth, then He is duty bound to chasten, correct, discipline, and train the church to bring Him pleasure and to fulfill His mission to win the lost.

I am quite convinced that God does afflict and discipline His people to rescue them from their own carnal pursuits, and to bring them into line with His plan and purpose.

> *"Does he who disciplines nations not punish? Does he who teaches man lack knowledge? The Lord knows the thoughts of man; he knows that they are futile. Blessed is the man you discipline, O Lord, the man you teach from your law; you grant him relief from days of trouble, til a pit is dug for the wicked."*
>
> Psalm 94:10-13 (NIV)

We can understand from these verses the **God punishes people for their wrong doing to teach them His ways** and to divert them from the consequences of their ways. This punishment from God, on His people, is fatherly chastening designed for their instruction, reformation, and improvement. Happy is the man who is educated by God. This education includes discipline and chastening.

If God would discipline nations He would certainly discipline His children when they get out of line. He wants His children to be good representatives of His teachings in the world. His instructions are, ***"Let your light so shine before man, that they may see your good works and glorify your Father in heaven."***

Matthew 5:16

Surely, if there was ever a time when the church needed to straighten up and send forth a steady light of example to a lost and dying world, it is today!

After Joshua died and all the generation who had witnessed the miracle works of God passed on,

"Another generation arose after them who did not know the Lord nor the work which He had done for Israel. And the anger of the Lord was hot against Israel. So He delivered them into the hands of plunderers who despoiled them; and He sold them into the hands of their enemies all around, so that they could no longer stand before their enemies."

Judges 2:7-14

This became a pattern for Israel. They would fall into sin and disobedience, then be disciplined by God, and then repent and return to God. This happened repeatedly until they were finally taken into captivity.

This disciplinary action, upon Israel, was under the direct supervision of God. He brought it upon them; (He was the one who implemented it), He controlled it; (He used it as a lesson to restore, not a tool to destroy), and He terminated it at His own discretion; (He didn't let it go longer than was absolutely necessary to accomplish His purpose.)

In Jeremiah 25:8-9, God foretells of a seventy-year exile of the nation of Judah in Babylon. We are given to know that this exile was under the afflicting hand of God, *"Because you have not heard My words."*

God has a way of dealing with His wayward children and often these dealings take on the form of severe affliction or judgment.

Consider the seventy-years of captivity of Judah under the hand of the Babylonians. The people were transported to a strange and troubling environment. They were humiliated with the memory of defeat, destruction, and displacement. Heavy taxes and burdensome services were imposed upon them, and anyone who would attempt to be faithful to the worship of Jehovah would be scorned, hindered, and targeted for special ridicule.

We know that among those taken into captivity were some faithful and true servants of God. Daniel, Shadrach, Meshack, and Abed-Nego were shining examples that God was at work even while Judah was suffering a humiliating defeat. These all shared in the deplorable conditions that existed in their day, yet, they emerged as blazing testimonies that God still had great plans for His people.

I wonder how the little children adjusted to life in Babylon. They say children are resilient and can adjust more easily to change than adults. However, children need support and security in order to build a healthy attitude of life. No doubt their outlook was threatened and their potential was challenged in the light of their circumstances. It was to the children that God made promises to remember them and to reverse their disgrace into delight and their lamentation into restoration. The future belonged to a new generation and God was preparing them for what was ahead.

I refer to these horrible experiences to help us realize what terrible and challenging times Judah went through before they would be ready for restoration and cleansing.

I think the church in America is no different than Judah. **We will never change our wayward tendencies until we are driven to our knees by painful afflictions** and impelled to humble ourselves, repent, and return to harmony with God and one another.

The whole purpose of the mortification of Judah in Babylon was to bring repentance and restoration to the nation. Even before the exile was implemented God promised:

"After seventy-years are completed in Babylon, I will visit you and perform my good word towards you, and cause you to return to this place. For I know the thoughts that I think toward you says the Lord, thoughts of peace and not evil, to give you a future, and a hope."
Jeremiah 29:10-11

God had plans for Judah and those plans projected beyond the painful captivity in Babylon. It took pain and disgrace to restore the joy and self-respect to a rebellious and backslidden people.

Lest we should restrict these disciplinary dealings to the Old Testament, let us be reminded of an ongoing principle of God found in Hebrews 10:28-29,

"Anyone who has rejected Moses' law dies without mercy on the testimony of two or three witnesses. Of how much worse punishment do you suppose, will he be thought worthy who has trampled the Son of God underfoot, counting the blood of the covenant by which he was sanctified a common thing, and insulting the Spirit of grace."

We must conclude from these verses that the New Testament principle of retribution is every bit as demanding as the Old Testament. If God would put Judah through exile to bring repentance and restoration, certainly He will disciple his wayward church and prepare her to be a better testimony before He returns to gather His church to be with Him forever.

We must understand that God allows bad things to happen to good people so those good people can become better people to fit His plan more perfectly. We also need to realize that all things, serving His purpose, work together for good, because He is behind the scene directing those things and bringing them to a beneficial end. (Romans 8:28)

God has a plan and is in the process of developing us to fit into His plan when and where and how He chooses. In Romans 9:20-24, Paul gives us an analogy of God forming Israel the way a potter forms his clay. The direct application of this is to Israel, but what applies to Israel applies to the church. What applies to the church applies to each of us as individuals since the church is made up of individuals.

We read in Romans 8:18-23 how the entire creation of God is waiting to see what God is going to bring forth from the troublesome times the world is passing through. Verse 19 indicates that a high level of that expectation is directed toward the revealing of the sons of God or the church.

It is our privilege to submit ourselves to God's plan and allow Him to mold and shape us to fit where He pleases. The fires of affliction and the adversities of life are the ingredients that God uses to design us for His plan.

Paul Orfalea was a kid with dyslexia, and had a school record that included the repetition of several grades, expulsions, and a stint with a school for retarded children. Plenty of Paul's teachers were convinced he was as dumb as a stump. One junior high school administrator told his mother, **"Maybe he could enroll in a good trade school and learn to lay carpet."**

In addition to all of this, kids called him "Kinko" because of his curly hair. From an outsider's point of view, Paul didn't have much going for him. He managed to graduate from high school with what he classified as, "a low D average." He then made his way through the University of Southern California with a similar lack of distinction. Rather than learning to lay carpet, in 1970, Paul started a small copy shop at an old hamburger stand. From the humble beginning, he turned a goofy nickname into an internationally known chain of stores. In 2000, Paul Orfalea, at the age of fifty-two, stepped down from the position of CEO of Kinko's. With multiple millions of dollars in his portfolio, Orfales credits his parents for encouraging him through such great adversity. To fellow dyslexics, Orfalea says, *"God gave you an advantage. So work with your strengths."* (5)

What an incredible story this is about turning our affliction into an advantage and excelling as a result. This is what Paul had in mind when he said, *"When I am weak, then I am strong."* II Corinthians 12:10 Paul was painfully aware that his thorn in the flesh was an adversity to him. With God's help he turned his inadequacy into victory. Realizing the advantage this gave him, Paul said;

*"Most gladly I will boast in my infirmities, that
the power of Christ may rest upon me."*

II Corinthians 12:9

With these things in mind we understand what the psalmist meant when he said, *"It is good for me that I have been afflicted, that I may learn your statutes."* Psalm 119:71 This was spoken in retrospect as he observed what had already happened. **It is much harder to realize the good of adversity while we are passing through it.** God, therefore, gives us some more scripture in Isaiah 43:2 to encourage us on our way,

"When you pass through the waters, I will be with you; And through the rivers, they shall not overflow you. (This gives us something to hold on to when we are passing through the deep waters.) ***When you walk through the fire, you shall not be burned."*** (This gives us something to hold on to when we are passing through the hot spots of life.)

What we have to understand is that we will always come through adversity and be a better person for it.

We tend to take for granted things that cost us nothing. We see this reflected in second generation children. I have heard it said by too many parents, *"My kids aren't going to have to go through life with the disadvantages I had to put up with."* The child is then given his every whim and grows up to be a spoiled brat that expects things to be handed to him on a silver platter. That parent, not realizing it, did the child a disservice by making life easy and non-threatening. The parent doesn't realize that adversity made them what they were and the lack of it made the child what they are today.

Who are the people who join protests against war and promote anti-war demonstrations? They are seldom the people who fought in war and helped to preserve our freedom. Those who have fought for freedom are the ones who sharply salute the flag with tears streaming down their faces singing, *"God bless America."*

Those who are participating in the protest, for the most part, are those who have never had to fight for freedom. They have grown up with freedom ringing from shore to shore and have never known first hand what it means to fight for freedom. **Those who have faced the adversity appreciate the victory.**

The greatest spiritual revivals today are taking place in countries where poverty, persecution, and pain pervade. I read monthly from Christian periodicals about the inhuman atrocities that are inflicted on these helpless people. They are driven to God because they have nowhere else to turn. These people are not detracted from their pursuit of God by the pleasures and pull of earthly attractions. Dependence on God becomes paramount.

We in America, on the other hand, have so many distractions we have a hard time fitting God into our bulging schedules. God is not our priority. He has to be squeezed into our schedule and then, if it is convenient, we will give Him some of our precious time.

We don't realize what we have lost. We wonder why we have so few of the marvelous miracles that we read about in the Bible and hear about in other countries. The truth is that we have at our disposal the material and means to do just about anything that we want to do in our own effort. We can do most of what we are doing without God's help. We're not pressed into the need for a miracle.

Need! Now that's an interesting word. It means to be in want of something necessary. We hate the word "need" when it applies to us. Needy people are those kinds of people for whom we collect food at Thanksgiving time or at Christmas. To be in need means all our desires are not being fulfilled. To be in need means we have to depend on someone else.

The Laodicean spirit is gripping us today. We are told of their spirit in Revelation 3:17, *"…I am rich and have become wealthy, and have need of nothing…"* That's about as deep as you can get in complacency and self-satisfaction. They were so independent they didn't need God. They didn't think of it as rejecting God, they thought of it as becoming successfully independent and capable of taking care of themselves. The problem was they left God out of the equation. That's easy to do when you have all you want.

This, to me, is why the "shaking loose" process is so necessary to serve God's purpose. It is a process that will leave us high and dry and dependent on God. We will be ready to cry out, *"We need you Lord, come and help us."* When He comes to us, we will be able to say with the Psalmist, *"It is good for me that I have been afflicted."*

Job was tried about as severely as anyone in the Bible, except Jesus. Job knew God put him in the refining fire. He confessed in Job 23:10, *"But He knows the way I take; When He has tested me, I shall come forth as gold."* Job didn't say this in retrospect; he said it in faith and anticipation. The process was painful and the struggle was intense. In the end, when he had more wealth, more children, more of everything, he could have said, *"It is good for me that I have been afflicted, for now my latter days are better that my beginning."*

God brings us through affliction to burn off the dross and make us more effective in our ministry for Him. II Timothy 2:20-21 addresses this truth very effectively:

> "But in a great house there are not only vessels of gold and silver, but also of wood and clay, some for honor and some for dishonor. Therefore if anyone cleanses himself from the latter, he will be a vessel for honor, sanctified and useful for the Master, prepared for every good work."

Eugene Peterson's, **"THE MESSAGE,"** gives an interesting slant to these verses:

"In a well-furnished kitchen there are not only crystal goblets and silver platters, but waste cans and compost buckets – some containers used to serve fine meals, others to take out the garbage. Become the kind of container God can use to present any and every kind of gift to his guests for their blessing."

The truth presented in these verses applies to both the church in general and also the true church of Jesus Christ. The vessels of gold and silver are the vessels of honor and are representative of the true church of sanctified believers. The vessels of wood and clay are the vessels of dishonor and are representative of those who make a profession but aren't sanctified for the Master's use. I like the way Peterson describes them, *"...waste cans and compost buckets...to take out the garbage."* That's exactly what some people are like. Their ears serve as a garbage can to deposit the latest gossip and carry it to the next garbage can. This would not be a very useful vessel in the House of God.

The wonderful truth to these verses is that vessels of dishonor can become vessels of honor by cleansing themselves. Verse 21, *"Therefore if anyone cleanses himself from the latter,* (garbage can vessels of dishonor) *he will be a vessel for honor, sanctified and useful for the Master, prepared for every good work."* This tells me there is hope for even the empty, carnal, dishonorable, garbage can, professing Christians if they will repent and be cleansed and sanctified for the Master's use.

The bottom line is we are, *"prepared for every good work."* The fiery trials and the shaking experiences are a preparation to make us more effective witnesses for the Master. He will do His part by shaking our world and burning our dross. We must join with Him and cleanse ourselves and set ourselves apart for His service. **In the end we will realize the affliction was good for us, for it equipped us for a more effective ministry.** This is one time when the end justifies the means.

Are You Ready?
Chapter 10

"Let us rejoice and be glad and give him glory! For the wedding of the Lamb has come, and his bride has made herself ready."
REVELATION 19:7 (NIV)

There was a young discus thrower who lived in the nineteenth century. This was in the days before professional trainers, so he developed his skills of throwing the discus on his own. He made his own discus from a description he read in a book. What he didn't know was that the discus used in competition was made of wood with an outer rim of iron. His was solid metal and weighed three of four times as much as those being used by his would-be challengers. This committed Scotsman marked out his field the distance of the current record throw and trained day and night to be able to match it. For nearly a year, he labored under the self-imposed burden of the extra weight, becoming very, very good. He reached the point at which he could throw his iron discus the record distance, maybe farther. He was ready.

The highlander traveled south to England for his first competition. When he arrived at the games, he was handed the official wooden discus – which he promptly threw like a tea saucer. He set a new record, a distance so far beyond those of his competitors that no one could touch him. For many years he remained the uncontested champion. (7)

This story teaches us that **laboring under adversity makes us better prepared to face the contest of spiritual opposition.** This, to me, is convincing proof that God sends us through adversity to equip us for better accomplishments. I think Job said it best:

"But He knows the way that I take; when He has tested me, I shall come forth as gold."

Job 23:10

We have to work through the tests and trials God sends our way. How we respond to adversity makes all the difference in the world about the outcome of our experience. If we complain, blame God, and become bitter we will fail the test, lose the lesson, and diminish our capability to improve. If we praise God, acknowledge His goodness, and submit to His assignment, we will profit from the lesson and enlarge our borders of influence.

God's word has instructed us as to what we must do to again become His Glorious Church prepared and ready for His coming. Personal and corporeal changes need to be made to experience His restoration. We deal with this topic in this final chapter of the book.

II Chronicles 7:14 is the paramount picture for preparation portrayed for us in the Old Testament:

"If my people who are called by My name will humble themselves, and pray and seek My face, and turn from their wicked ways, then I will hear from heaven, and will forgive their sin and heal their land."

The first condition God sets down for us in this scripture is to, "humble ourselves." If we fail to humble ourselves God has ways to humble us. However, He gives us first chance to humble ourselves, which is usually easier to take than having outside help to accomplish the task. A good description for humility is:

Have more that thou showest;
Speak less that thou knowest. (2)

Humility is an attitude that gets the attention of God. Isaiah 66:2 (NIV), *"This is the one I esteem: he who is humble and contrite in spirit, and trembles at my word."* If humility will cause God to esteem us, then we should pursue this requirement with enthusiastic desire.

Next, we are told **we must "pray and seek His face."** Every Christian knows they should pray more, we just don't follow through on it. When we "seek His face," however, we pray with a special focus on Him rather than on His blessings. We also pray with a higher degree of intensity. Jeremiah 29:13, *"And you will seek Me and find Me, when you search for Me with all your heart."* This is not a feeble, fumbling prayer for Him, it is an intense interest in Him as our objective.

Then we are to *"turn from our wicked ways."* **Confession is not enough**. Also, saying such things as, *"Smile, God loves you!"* or *"I'm okay, you're okay!"* or *"Every road leads to heaven,"* doesn't cut it. The simple message is, *"REPENT."* There must be a powerful repentance that results in going in a new direction. That's what repentance means, a 180 degree turn around.

We are not always aware of any wickedness in us, so we should ask God to show us where we might have to change. We are reminded again that this is what David prayed, *"Search me, O God, and know my heart: try me, and know my thoughts, And see if there be any wicked way in me, and lead me in the way everlasting."* Psalm 139:23-24 (KJV) This is a daring prayer, but when it is answered it can turn our lives around.

The time has come to repent, face the music, remove the clutter, and become sensitive to the Holy Spirit. Those daring prayers must be prayed if we are to change. We need passion in our prayers like Joel instructed, *"Consecrate a fast, call a sacred assembly; Gather the elders and all the inhabitants of the land into the house of the Lord your God, and cry out to the Lord."* Joel 1:14 (This is not a call to a generic prayer we have memorized; it is a call to a passionate prayer with stirred emotions erupting from a spirit filled heart.) This is the *"effectual fervent prayer of a righteous man."* James 5:16

God has already done the groundwork; we must now join hands with Him and exercise our will to respond to the prompting of the Holy Spirit. We can't do it all, and God won't do it all. We must work together to orchestrate a manifestation of God's power.

We often find ourselves in the state of mind that Paul describes in Romans 7:18, *"...for to will is present with me, but how to perform what is good I do not find."* The answer to this quandary comes when Paul moves into Romans 8 and teaches about the work of the Spirit. Our will and God's Spirit must work together to accomplish spiritual progress.

I like to illustrate this truth by showing the need for two keys to open a safe deposit box. You have a key and the bank has a key. Your key alone will not open the box, and the bank's key alone will not open it either. Both keys must be inserted and turned to open the box. Our will is one key to spiritual development and God's Spirit is the other key. We can't do it alone, and God won't do it alone. Both keys must be used.

This principle applies to any of the directives given in the scriptures: resist the devil; set your mind on things above; draw near to God; be holy; make disciples of all nations; and love your neighbor. When we exercise our will to obey God's word, God takes reciprocal action and enables us to follow through.

Before our will can function effectively it must be sanctified and surrendered to God. Jesus surrendered His will to the Father when He prayed in the Garden of Gethsemane, *"O my Father, if it is possible, let this cup pass from Me; nevertheless, not as I will, but as You will."* Matthew 26:39

The un-surrendered will, exercised in the lusts of the flesh, will lead us into sin and confusion. The surrendered will, exercised in the power of the Holy Spirit, will purify our steps and enable us to walk in the light of His word. It is necessary for us to exercise our surrendered will to get ourselves ready for the bridegroom.

Why should we feel we must go into a preparation stage as we approach the coming of the Lord? Is it not enough that we know our sins are forgiven, and we are on our way to heaven? This would probably be an adequate aspiration for many Christians who are content with the ordinary and willing to accept the familiar. However, Christians who are not satisfied with the status quo realize that there is always more to attain in spiritual development.

Paul realized this for his own life when he wrote, *"Not that I have already attained, or am already perfected; but I press on, that I may lay hold of that for which Christ Jesus has also laid hold of me."* Philippians 3:12 Paul was a seasoned veteran when he penned these words and was still reaching out for more of God. He was not content with what had been, he was looking forward to what could yet be.

Solomon gives us a picture of this in Proverbs 4:18, *"But the path of the just is like the shining sun, That shines ever brighter unto the perfect day."* The church is not going to flicker and fade out of the picture in the last days, but it is going to increase and blossom forth as His coming materializes.

Peter supports this concept in II Peter 1:5-11:

"...giving all diligence, add to your faith virtue, to virtue knowledge, to knowledge self-control, to self-control perseverance, to perseverance godliness, to godliness brotherly kindness, and to brotherly kindness love. For if these things are yours and abound, you will be neither barren nor unfruitful in the knowledge of our Lord Jesus Christ. For he who lacks these things is shortsighted, even to blindness, and has forgotten that he was cleansed from his old sins. Therefore, brethren, be even more diligent to make your call and election sure, for if you do these things you will never stumble; for so an entrance will be supplied to you abundantly into the everlasting kingdom of our Lord and Savior Jesus Christ."

According to Peter there is a whole lot of "adding to" that needs to be done before we enter the "everlasting kingdom." And when we do, it will be an "abundant entrance" not an anemic evacuation.

I hope you can see my rationale now for suggesting we have a job on our hands if we are going to prepare ourselves to be that glorious church without spot or wrinkle that will rise to meet our Conquering Savior.

There is a long list of requirements that I could suggest for us to follow if we are going to be ready for His coming. The problem with making a list of spiritual requirements is that you end up in a legalistic quagmire. **It is more than a matter of righteousness; it is a matter of relationship.** We have to build a relationship with God so strong that we will be sensitive to anything that would disconnect us from God.

"Enoch walked with God; and he was not, for God took him."
Genesis 5:24

We don't know too much about Enoch except, **"*before he was taken he had this testimony, that he pleased God.*"** Hebrews 11:5 It should be our goal to walk with God and please Him, like Enoch, that we might be ready for Him to take us. When we walk with God we will build a relationship with Him that will make us sensitive to please Him.

Preparing ourselves for the coming of the Lord is only part of the story. The other part is reaching the lost and making productive disciples of them. The church is failing miserably in this task. Many of the churches, where I have been called to minister recently, have had no new converts for years. The main reason for this is that there is no concentrated training to accomplish this task. People are not inclined to perform a task they are not trained to execute and challenged to achieve.

George Barna gives some good strategies for producing disciples in his book, **"GROWING TRUE DISCIPLES."** He says, *"The end goal of disciples is both personal and corporate. The personal goal is to live a life worthy of the name "Christian." The corporate goal is to introduce other people to Jesus, help them to accept Him as their Savior, and enable them to live the life worthy of someone known as a Christian. The Great Commission is not primarily about evangelism, it is about discipleship: 'Therefore go and make disciples of all nations.' (Matthew 28:19) An individual who does not reproduce themselves in Christ is not truly a disciple since he does not exhibit the selfless love of the Master."* (4)

Barna is on target; **we reproduce ourselves in the people we disciple**. We can't expect them to go beyond our example since we are the models to be followed. That means we will have to be ready for the coming of the Lord if we are going to disciple them to be ready.

There may be someone who is reading this book who doesn't know God in a personal life changing experience. I ask you, if you were to stand before God and have Him ask you, *"Why should I let you into my heaven, what would you say?"* I want you to know you can be sure you are ready to stand before God and give the right answer to this question.

It all begins when you realize you have sinned and failed to keep God's commandments: *"for all have sinned and fall short of the glory of God."* Romans 3:23 You have to realize that you are lost before you can be found, otherwise you will resent anyone who would suggest that you change direction.

Next, you have to understand the consequence of your sin; *"For the wages of sin is death, but the gift of God is eternal life in Christ Jesus our Lord."* Romans 6:23 A wage is a payment you receive for what you have done. On the positive side, you work at a job and receive a wage for services rendered. On the negative side, there is a payday coming when you will receive payment for the sins you have committed. A gift is something you receive by the good grace of the giver. You don't work for it, nor do you pay for it. The reason we don't have to pay for this gift is because, *"while we were still sinners, Christ died for us."* Romans 5:8 This means He took the penalty for our sins upon Himself when He died on the cross; He paid the ransom for the sins that held us captive.

There is action we can take to apply this salvation to our personal lives: *"If we confess our sins, He is faithful and just to forgive us our sins and to cleanse us from all unrighteousness."*

I John 1:9

Now you know why He can forgive your sins. Are you ready to ask Him to come into your life and make you ready for His coming?

Soon the announcement will come forth, **"Ready or not, here I come!"** Are you ready for this announcement?

Resources Used

Footnotes:
(1) Taken from 1001 Humorous Illustrations for Public Speaking, by Michael Hodgin.
Copyright 1994 by Michael Hodgin.
Used by permission of the Zondervan Publishing House
Grand Rapids, MI 49530
(2) Taken from 1002 Humorous Illustrations for Public Speaking by Michael Hodgin.
Copyright 2004 by Michael Hodgin.
Used by permission of the Zondervan Publishing House,
Grand Rapids, MI 49530
(3) 1500 Illustrations for Biblical Preaching
by Michael P. Green
Copyright 1982, 1985, 1989
Baker Books, a division of Baker Publishing Group,
Grand Rapids, MI 49516
Used by permission
(4) Growing True Disciples
George Barna
Copyright 2001 –
Random House/Waterbrook Press, Colorado Springs, Colorado 80920
(5) McHenry's Stories for the Soul (Exerpts on pages 5, 6, 8, 168, 170, 205, and 264 were taken from this book by Raymond McHenry.)
Copyright 2001 by Hendrickson Publishers, Inc.
Peabody, Massachusetts 01961
Used by permission. All rights reserved.
(6) A Glorious Church – Words & Music (1892)
Ralph Erskine Hudson (1843-1901)
Used by permission

(7) Perfect Illustrations for Every Topic and Occasion
Copyright 2002 – Christianity Today International
Tyndale House Publishers, Wheaton, Illinois
- Page 46, Jim Davis, pastor, Silverdale, WA
- Page 61, Mary Chambers, Leadership
- Page 124, John Ellredge, The Sacred Romance (Nelson, 1997)
- Page 134, Barry Marritt, Toledo, OH
- Page 254, Brett Kays

(8) The Barna Group, Ltd.
"Morality Continues to Decay" Articles taken from the Internet:
www.barna.org
Barna Updates 11/03/03, 12/15/04, 6/9/05
1957 Eastman Ave., Ste. B
Ventura, California 93003
Used by permission

(9) Our Daily Bread
Copyright 2005 – RBC Ministries, Grand Rapids, Michigan 49501
Citation: David McCasland
Used by permission

About The Author

Robert L. Bradley was born in Flint, Michigan in 1934. His family finally settled in Boyne City, Michigan due to the work situation for his father. His wife, Virginia was born in Beaver Falls, Pennsylvania.

When Robert was called to preach the gospel at the age of 19 years, he knew precisely that the particular call was to "prepare God's people" for Christ's return.

God, in His providence, brought Virginia (Ginny) Morar into his life while both were attending Eastern Bible Institute now known as Valley Forge Christian College in Pennsylvania. They married after graduation in 1956.

They began pastoring in a small Home Mission's church in Ithaca, Michigan, and later became assistant pastor to Rev. Ted Ness of Berea Tabernacle in Detroit, Michigan. From there they went into 2 years of evangelism ministry that included Michigan, Pennsylvania, Ohio, New York, and Ontario, Canada. They pastored for 8 years in Latrobe, Pennsylvania followed by 9 years in Saginaw, Michigan, and then lastly they spent over 19 years in Ferndale, Michigan before retiring from full-time pastoring in October, 1997.

Robert & Virginia became a team with corresponding interests, and together they have faithfully sought to fulfill this mission that God laid upon their hearts. Both ministers, they sing together and have recorded a CD of their special songs.

This book could never have come to fruition without Virginia's untiring attention to small details and her faithful support and encouragement to this project.

Now retired from full time pastoral ministry, the Bradley's reside in Grayling, Michigan where they still seek to provide direction and encouragement to the churches in the area. They have two children, Brenda and Bruce, along with eight grandchildren.

Printed in the United States
42647LVS00007B/238-339